The Dragon and the GOAT

THE
DRAGON
AND THE GOAT

How to Turn Fear
Into an Ally and
Design a Life
of Profit, Joy,
and Fulfillment

Rebecca Mountain

NEW YORK

LONDON • NASHVILLE • MELBOURNE • VANCOUVER

The Dragon and the GOAT

How to Turn Fear Into an Ally and Design a Life of Profit, Joy, and Fulfillment

© 2025 Rebecca Mountain

Published in New York, New York, by Morgan James Publishing. Morgan James is a trademark of Morgan James, LLC. www.MorganJamesPublishing.com

Proudly distributed by Publishers Group West®

Morgan James
BOGO™

A **FREE** ebook edition is available for you
or a friend with the purchase of this print book.

CLEARLY SIGN YOUR NAME ABOVE

Instructions to claim your free ebook edition:
1. Visit MorganJamesBOGO.com
2. Sign your name CLEARLY in the space above
3. Complete the form and submit a photo
   of this entire page
4. You or your friend can download the ebook
   to your preferred device

ISBN 9781636983950 paperback
ISBN 9781636983967 ebook
Library of Congress Control Number:
2024941121

Cover & Interior Design by:
Christopher Kirk
www.GFSstudio.com

Morgan James is a proud partner of Habitat for Humanity Peninsula
and Greater Williamsburg. Partners in building since 2006.

Get involved today! Visit: www.morgan-james-publishing.com/giving-back

To Marc, my "everything" and our kids. This is all for you.

CONTENTS

The Crash 1

How We Got Here 5

    A Different Ending 8

How to Get Your GOAT 11

    And So the Story Goes (On and On and On) 12

    Book 1: The Dragon and the GOAT 14

    Book 2: How to Shrink Your Dragon 15

    Book 3: Stepping into Your GOAT Life 15

BOOK 1, PART 1: TIME TO MEET YOUR DRAGON 17

How Your Dragon Wins 23

    When the "We Only Use 10% of Our Brain" Myth Is True 23

    Tests, Fear, and Brain Freeze 27

    Our (Dis)comfort Zone – "Familiar" Is Not Always "Good" 29

    Baby Bird Syndrome 31

    How Making a "Big Leap" Makes You Sick –and Why That's Awesome . . . 33

    Comparison Culture (Your Internal Cancel Culture!) 35

    Procrastination, Avoidance, and Inconsistency. 38

    Making Excuses and Avoiding Disappointment. 40

    Pain Identities: Frozen in Time 43

    Pervasive Unhappiness. 46

The Undoing Process. 48

Do What You're Supposed to Do. 49

Wired for Negativity. 52

Fake Commitment 53

"It's Fine" (No, It's Not) 55

Deflection (Not Taking Compliments) .57

Name the Dragon 59

A Final Word About Your Dragon. 62

BOOK 1, PART 2: ARE YOU LIVING YOUR GOAT LIFE?. 65

How to Know If You're Living Your GOAT Life 67

What Living a GOAT Life Means 70

Feeling Limitless 71

There's a GOAT in Each of Us 72

Talents and Skills 73

Living Life on Your Terms. 75

Feelings and Freak-Outs 77

Impact over Income 78

Invite – Don't Chase – Success (Impact over Income Cont'd) 80

Growth Mindsets 81

Personal Standard of Excellence. 83

Living with Purpose on Purpose 85

Driven by Happiness. 86

Be 1% Better. 87

The Only Competitor in the Room. 89

Fueled – Not Frightened – by Your Dark Side 90

Failure Is a Competitive Advantage 91

Do the Work Most Won't 92

Star Connections. 93

Necessary Endings. 94

The BodyMind Connection 95

Downtime Is Highly Valued 96

Be Intentional with Your Time 97

Are You Living Your GOAT Life? 99

BOOK 2: HOW TO SHRINK YOUR DRAGON 101
How to Shrink Your Dragon 105
    Naming and Claiming Your Emotions. 106
    Processing the Physical Energy of Emotions 111
    Regular Mindfulness Meditation. 113
    Self-Worth and the Root of Inconsistency 116
    Breathing Deeply 117
    Gratitude and Appreciation. 119
    The Story Changing Process 121
    The Assumption Challenging Process 124
    Eliminating Your Pain Identities 127
    From Filth to Fertilizer 131
    Happiness Triggers 134
    The Danger of "Why" 137
    Don't Be a "Hero" 138
    The Language of Commitment 139
    Improve Sleep 140
    What Will You Do Now? 141

BOOK 3: STEPPING INTO YOUR GOAT LIFE. 143
How to Feed Your GOAT. 149
    What Makes You Happy? 150
    Living Life on Your Terms. 155
    Clarifying Your GOAT Self. 156
    My Personal Best Cheat Sheet. 158
    Creating Your Purpose Statement 159
    Impact over Income – The Strategy. 162
    Fostering a Growth Mindset 165
    Confidence & Motivation Come After Action. 167
    From Goals to Actions – Replace Decisions with Instructions 168
    Setting Boundaries – Okay and Not Okay. 173

Superpowers and Dark Sides 178

The Dark Side. 181

How to Get Work off Your Plate: The ADORE Method 183

Being Intentional with Your Time. 186

The Power of Star Beginnings 190

Necessary Conversations – and Necessary Endings 193

Taking Care of Your Health and Well-Being .198

About the Author 201

THE CRASH

I locked the front door and looked at my watch by the light of the street lamps. I was late. It was already 6:30 am, and I was supposed to be at a meeting by then. It was a rather unorthodox time, but the project was urgent, and we needed every spare minute. I saw my breath in the cold morning air as I hurried down the steps.

I jumped into my modest silver sedan and felt a pang of loss at not having my old five-speed. It felt more like *driving*. I double-checked to make sure I had all my files and my computer, and hit the gas.

I raced down the four-lane road to the highway. Only a few cars. Good. I sped past people on their way to work, going just over 100 km/hr in a 60 zone. I didn't care. I was late. That's all I could think about. As I approached the on-ramp to the highway, I slowed slightly. I'd lived in the area for nearly fifteen years, and felt like I knew how to take it. Speed was my thing. I could control it, even if cops thought it was a bad idea. I'd just paid off my ninth speeding ticket that year, so maybe I was a little too quick. Whatever. I was late. I would worry about slowing down tomorrow. I entered the curve and realized too late that this one was a little tighter than the other ones. I pulled quickly to the right, and that's when I felt the back end slide out. I'd been in a slide before, so I let go of the wheel, took my foot off the gas, and waited for the car to straighten out. Except it didn't.

I had failed to see the glisten of black ice on the dark pavement. I continued to turn, facing the wrong direction, and edging toward the embankment. I was backward now, staring at a row of oncoming lights in the dark morning. And then I went over.

I felt my speed pick up as I flew over the edge. I was still going about 60 km/hr, and as the car caught air I was suspended, everything going absolutely silent. When I hit the ground, it was at an angle. My tires exploded, and I was hurtled down the 30-foot embankment onto my roof, my car landing oddly on the six-lane road. The top of the car crushed me against the steering wheel. Thankfully, the air bags did not deploy. I would have been dead in an instant.

I held the wheel tight, trying to keep my face from scraping on the fast-moving pavement just millimeters away. The windows had exploded, and glass was cascading everywhere, hitting me in the face and neck, scarring my hands as I desperately held on. I felt dirt and oil spray on my face as the car continued its relentless pace, spinning, sliding. It felt like forever, and yet in an instant, it was over. There I was, upside down in my car, in the dark, on a busy highway, facing the wrong way — and I was alive.

For most people, that simple revelation is enough to sing and dance to a song of thanks. For me, it was deeper. I had been thinking seriously about leaving the cult-like church I grew up in, but leaving wasn't something you were supposed to do. The leaders liked to scare you by telling you that if you even *thought* about leaving, you would die, either by cancer or a car crash.

This was my car crash. And I did not die. *They were wrong.*

In that pivotal moment, my entire life changed. I opened my new skylight, which used to be the passenger door, and jumped down to the road. I had blocked the entire highway, so cars had to pass on the shoulder. As I shook the glass from my hair and picked the dirt from my ears, I thought again, *They were wrong.*

And if they were wrong, and I did not die even though I *should* be dead for wanting to escape the church … what else were they lying about?

Standing at the side of the road, waiting for the tow truck to right my now-flattened car, I started to question everything that I had been accepting in my life. What else was I doing, like a "good girl," that I hated, or that made me feel small and insignificant? The answers started to pile up, and before long, I had a list that started to make me question my entire existence.

Looking back now, I know that I lived my life like I thought I was supposed to. I did nothing to make myself happy, or that would make me feel empowered or proud of myself. Things like that were considered "prideful" and therefore wrong, so I had trained myself to avoid any situation that would make me feel good about myself. In my recent studies, I've come to the conclusion that most of the world lives this way, to various degrees.

What drives us to live like this? For me, that crash was my wake-up call, and I had to make a change or the next one would seal the deal. I had two small boys, whom I loved more than life — so I had to do something, urgently, to put my life back in order.

In this way, I faced my "Dragon," the part of my brain that makes me stay "safe," living according to the rules, never sticking my neck out lest I end up making a mistake. By the end of that year, I had left the church, gotten a divorce, and lost my job. (I was working for folks in the church. They did not see things my way.) I was on my own, terrified, but happy to be free.

And yet, I was not free. In the years that followed, I dragged that Dragon with me everywhere. I had physically left situations and relationships that hurt me, but that pain was still in there, festering and keeping me from living my true life.

In this book, I will show you how I came to find my GOAT — my Greatest of All Time. I live life on my terms now, in relationships that give me what I need, without fear that I will be made small. I do work that matters to me and to my clients. I can see my future clearly and feel that what I'm doing now is what I was destined to do.

Destiny and manifestation are beautiful dreams, but without action and clarity, they fade and die. If you want your Dragon to loosen its hold on your heart, and you want to tap into your greatness, then you've come to the right place. I aim to show you how, explaining in detail how you got to where you are, and then map out a path to your own GOAT life.

But first, here's a little story about how we get into a situation where our Dragon rules our hearts and minds, instead of what truly makes us happy and fulfilled.

HOW WE GOT HERE

In the beginning, the Dragon was small, weak, and almost always defeated by the GOAT. The human in which they lived was small, full of curiosity, and had a complete disregard for risk or failure. She just wandered everywhere, touching things, tasting things. Going places where the risk of injury, judgment, shame, or danger roved wildly; and it drove the Dragon nuts.

But the GOAT loved it! She did what she wanted with blatant disregard for what anyone thought. She'd sing, dressed as a banana, surrounded by animals she named after her favorite apples.

She climbed trees, pretending to see to the ends of the earth. She was captain of her own ship, sailing into the Bermuda Triangle. She was a tiger, creeping up on prey at sunset. She dreamed, believing she could be and do anything.

This went on for years, with the GOAT frolicking annoyingly around the Dragon as the little human invented, danced, sang and played, flaunting her freedom and mocking the Dragon. But the Dragon knew all it had to do was wait. Its time would come.

And soon it did.

The human became a teen, and emotions started running high. The Dragon flexed and shook itself off. Creeping out of its cave where it had been waiting out the bouncing GOAT-filled days, it sniffed the air. It felt fresh and ripe. It was time.

Emotions started to feed the Dragon — the extreme highs, the devastating lows. They were delicious! Nutritious! Wondrous! Its claws grew strong and gripped her heart tightly. It grabbed her throat to make her anxiety a physical thing, feasting on the emotions that made her heart beat so fast. So fast. It had so much to work with now: confusing the human by telling her to fit in but still stand out. That she could do what she wanted but only within the lines drawn for her. It confounded her by magnifying the cruelty of the world and the pain of loss and rejection. She shrank back; the world wasn't safe anymore. It hurt.

"Luscious!" thought the Dragon. "Delicious!"

The Dragon feasted on these feelings, finally able to rein in the human and show her just how dangerous the world really was. When the human found pictures online of her friends partying without her, the Dragon threw the biggest pity party it could cook up. Her body flooded with anger, resentment, and fury; and oh, how sweet it was! The pity party lasted for three days before the Dragon stopped feeding her stories about how much she didn't

matter, but in those three days, the Dragon doubled in size.

The GOAT was getting worried. No more jumping. No more dancing. Its size shrank with every successive blow the Dragon landed on the human, making her feel shame, guilt, and fear. So much fear. So much judgment, rejection, and failure. These were to be avoided at all costs now.

"Stay safe," whispered the Dragon. "Don't go out there. Those people aren't your friends. Imagine what they're saying about you right now! Go online, and see if they're going without you again. That'll make you mad but keep you home."

And so, the tables turned. During those teenage years, the human started holding back. She tried to gauge what other people wanted her to do and how they wanted her to act, and she did her best to live accordingly. She masked her feelings. She lied about how she truly felt.

She tried so hard to live up to everyone's expectations but constantly found herself coming up short. She was disappointed by others who didn't read her mind and live up to what *she* believed was right. Nothing was good. Nothing was going according to her plans. Her resentment grew, but she shoved it down.

After what felt like one crushing blow after another, she learned how to avoid pain. She learned to choke back her fear. She took instructions from others instead of making decisions. She stopped feeling because it hurt too much. She went through the motions of life but did not feel it.

She toed the line. She played it safe. She went to school. Got good grades. Went to college, then got a job, determined to fit in and not stand out. Had friends that came and went. Toe the line. Just toe the line.

When boyfriends broke up with her, the Dragon reminded her of all the *other* times people had chosen to leave her, so she'd feel that much more depressed ... and the Dragon kept her safe. "Stop that dangerous dating thing," whispered the Dragon. "Find someone who comes with NO risks attached." The Dragon helped her see only those "safe" men by making them the ONLY men she ever saw. (There were others who would probably have been perfect ... but the Dragon made her blind to them, one of its particularly powerful talents. They came in and out of her life, but she never even knew they were there.)

She married the simple man who told her what to do and protected her from decisions. They had kids. They worked. They sometimes made love, and it was okay. She was lonely and sad but figured that this is what life was like. Everyone seemed lonely and sad, so who was she to complain?

And she accepted it.

By the time she was in her thirties, her GOAT was so small that it took effort to find. The Dragon built it a cage, and the GOAT stayed in there — quiet and still. The girl turned gray inside, devoid of color and shape. She stopped doing the things she loved. Music that used to thrill her and make her dance. She stopped reading books that used to take her to faraway places. They were full of people who were kind, beautiful, dashing…These people didn't exist, and she became frustrated when she compared the people in her life with those on the page. So, she gave the books away.

She became small.

She had no depth, no smell, and no passion. Love fell apart. The children grew up and moved away. The job was just a job. It paid the bills but nothing else.

She retired, still alone and not well. She joined a retirement community, trying to find a connection. And maybe she did, but she never learned what it truly felt like, so when someone tried to connect, she scurried away. *That is not safe. It brings pain. Retreat! Retreat!* Life is full of regret. She spent her remaining years in an "if only …" world.

A DIFFERENT ENDING ...

I actually depressed myself writing that story. Parts of it were from my own past, and that feeling of losing color and shape can happen without even noticing until one day you look in the mirror and wonder who's staring back at you.

The good news is that the next chapters of your story do not have to be so bleak. It's a choice that you have to make, just like the character in the story above could have gone down a different path.

What if, midway through those early adult years, when the rational part of her brain finally formed itself (it came online at about twenty-five), ... she chose instead to feed the GOAT once again? There's no way to make the teen years fun, but once you've run that gauntlet, the opportunities for a fulfilling life multiply.

To choose to dance. To sing. To love and be loved. To be rejected and see it as a gift — a lesson on how to make the next relationship more beautiful and more in line with what made her happy. Not settling for "good enough," knowing that it never is, and never will be. To not try to "*fix*" a partner, but find one that already *fits*.

And what if, instead of looking for happiness elsewhere, she found it within herself and dipped her entire body into that wellspring of joy and validation and love? As she dove into this fountain, she found her GOAT, brought it to the surface, and rode that beautiful beast into the sunset as the Dragon watched, shrinking ever so slowly behind them.

Imagine how life would look for her then. It's your turn to turn the lens upon your own world. What do you see?

This is a business book. This is a psychology book. This is whatever you need it to be. I am no expert, and the stories I share are from my personal experiences, work I've done with clients, books I've read — even the animated movies I love.

The question you must ask yourself every day is: *Who's winning your war: the Dragon or the GOAT?* For most of us, the Dragon rules the roost. We have learned that we risk massive exposure, ridicule, rejection, and more if we show the world what we're really capable of, so we keep it hidden, lest the cruelty of the world be turned upon us.

But what if you learned not to *care* about how the world sees you? What if the world is more welcoming than you think? And what if people are fascinated by how you run your business — not critical? Or what if you simply choose whom to love — and how you choose to show it — and tell everyone with an opinion about it to stick it where the sun don't shine?

What if you spent every day incandescently happy (my favorite line from *Pride and Prejudice*!)? You just shine your little face off, every day. You jump out of bed, so excited about getting going that you can hardly contain yourself.

Not very long ago, I would contemplate the risks of not getting out of bed — my business failing, my family ebbing away. Until one day, I decided to shrink my Dragon, to take it on once and for all, and build my life from my GOAT-ness. We all have this power, and there is more strength within to win this war than you think. If you're ready to start your engine, heat up your life, and generate a light that no one will ever dim or extinguish, build things no one will ever take away from you, feel whole and full and that you matter in every way, then I welcome you to the fight of your life.

There is no fight more worth your time and energy than this. Buckle up. We have a Dragon to wrestle!

HOW TO GET YOUR GOAT

The first time I got fired, I was four weeks pregnant. I was working for an organization that thrived on fear. Every six months or so, they'd throw everyone into a pot, reassign roles, and fire from five to fifty people. The number of folks who got canned varied, but there were mornings when what used to be Bob's desk was now occupied by some chick named Alice. It was unsettling. Being only four weeks into my pregnancy, I hadn't told anyone that I was expecting. Having a kid can be your career death knell if you're a woman, especially if you're not working in a supportive workplace (and I wasn't). Maternity leave in Canada had just gone from six months to twelve, and some employers weren't happy about it. My plan was to keep my pregnancy a secret for as long as I could.

One Monday in February, a mandatory company meeting was called. The day before this sure-to-be-fun-fest, I realized that it coincided with my first ultrasound, something I could not miss. I found my manager and explained that I simply could not go. Reading her face, I could see that she was miffed because I knew these mandatory meetings were tantamount to religion for this place. So, I dropped the bomb.

"I'm pregnant, Andrea. I can't go because it's my first ultrasound," I said, standing in the hallway between the marketing horror show that I worked in and accounting.

Her face went white, which at the time I thought was rather odd. Most people offer congratulations, but then again, this place wasn't typical. I'm pretty sure they ate their young. She said nothing and walked away. I couldn't figure her out, so I went back to my desk and went about my work, putting the conversation out of my mind.

About an hour later, I felt a tap on my shoulder. It was Andrea. HR would like to "have a chat." I don't know if you've ever been fired, but when HR taps you to "*have a chat*," it's not good, my friend. Not good.

My body immediately went into full panic mode. My mind started racing: What did I do? Who did I piss off? Did I mess something up that bad? Are there more people getting the boot today than just me? *And what am I going to do to find another job???? FFS I'm four weeks pregnant!*

By the time I reached the boardroom, my mind was whirling. I felt faint. Companies don't hire pregnant women, I told myself. I was screwed. And along with that sense of doom was that all-too-familiar feeling that everything I did was awful. I was awful. I was a failure. I would never amount to anything. The shame was already creeping up the back of my neck. I wasn't smart or good enough to keep this job (which wasn't hard), so what are my chances of getting anything decent *while pregnant,* etc. etc. etc.

As we sat around the table, me, my manager, and three human resources people, discussing the fact that I was getting the boot, and how I'd get my things to leave quietly, the only thing I managed to squeak out was, "Isn't it interesting that the day I get fired is the day I told Andrea I was pregnant." More white faces. They didn't like that. *Screw you guys*, I thought. *I'm going to milk this for all it's worth.*

So, I sued them, and I got double the severance, found a job in three weeks, and away I went. Surely, that horrible experience was in my past and the future would be bright and sunny. Truth be told, I would be fired two more times after that, but let's not get ahead of ourselves. More on that later!

AND SO THE STORY GOES

This story repeats itself by varying degrees of intensity, every day, all day. One day we're in a panic, the next day we're chilling and having a good time. Other days, it feels like we're stuck in neutral. We seesaw our way through life, feeling buffeted by what the world throws at us.

We read faces. We anticipate outcomes. We try to fit in and stand out at the same time but in the least offensive, aggressive way possible. We try (and fail) to predict how things will go and what people will say. We hold back and then berate ourselves for our cowardice. We wish, we want, and we hope — but we don't often actually do anything about it. Our bodies become awash in various sensations, from positive to devastating. Our brains try to make lightning-fast calculations to protect ourselves, keep us safe, stave off disaster, and find a place to belong, often at a great personal and spiritual cost.

For most of my life, I figured I was at the world's mercy, and my brain took up the cause. I seemed to react to things so quickly that I just went with it and tried to hold on for the ride, trusting that I was being true to myself, when in truth I was letting my Dragon take the wheel. Turns out, blindly trusting my brain to tell me what to do is both stupid and unnecessary. I've discovered that we actually have the ability to *control* how we react to things, instead of shooting our mouths off or becoming unnecessarily anxious. We can even make decisions on how we want to feel about things. We become aware of our powers, and what's more, we can physically change our brain to make this newfound control permanent. Eureka!

I am by no means the first person to have made this discovery. To be honest, I feel incredibly late to the game, like the kid who shows up to a party already in full swing. But this is my book, and I get to be excited about my discoveries, the ones I make precisely whenever I make them! I say this because some people may read this book and feel dumb for not knowing these simple things — but you don't know what you don't know, and beating yourself up feeds the Dragon, which is the opposite of what we're after.

To understand more about how to take back control of your gray matter, manage your emotions, and get insanely happy and successful, you need to dig into the research. But fear not, my friends: I've done that heavy lifting for you. There are mountains of books and white papers you can read to dig even further into what this book presents, and I encourage you to do so. Through-out, you'll hear about books I love that have changed the way I look at myself and the world around me, so go ahead and buy them!

In this book, you'll get stories that you can relate to and stats you can believe in. I'll be handing out strategies that you can use every day, all day, to take control of your life, your emotions, and the way you see the world. Some things you can start using while you're reading this book. Others will require you to put this delightful book down and do some work. I encourage you to get a notebook and pen ready and keep them with you as you read, to jot down a thought, inspiration, or something you're going to do differently to move your life in line with the GOAT within.

The book is split into three sections:

BOOK 1: THE DRAGON AND THE GOAT

How do you know if the Dragon or the GOAT is winning?

In many cases, we're not aware of the war that is being waged and even less conscious of which side is winning. In the first part of this book, I will explain several situations so you will know whether the Dragon has a grip on your heart, or your GOAT is bounding around, free to roam.

You'll learn how to know when the Dragon is winning, and the situations in which you may find yourself that allow this malevolent beast to direct your life.

We'll then explore how to know if you're living a GOAT life or not. You'll be able to gauge how closely your life resembles a GOAT way of living, working, and going about relationships.

The idea with Book 1 is for you to see which side has the upper hand, and to become aware of how you can start to make some changes. There is an urgency to adjust your life, because if happiness is not pervasive in every minute of your day, then there's a problem. Someone recently told me that my drive to be "happy" cannot be possible. He had accomplished many of his original goals and felt that happiness was not for him. It just wasn't out there. After some back and forth, and a lot of resistance on his part on how to generate these awesome feelings and experiences in his life, we landed on an agreement: he would at least start telling himself that "happiness is possible" — and take it from there, see what happens.

Happiness is not sheer bliss and joy every minute of every day. It's a feeling that you're always in control, you know what you want (and get it or ask for it), and your boundaries are solid. This is how I live my life, and yet I'm always working hard on being even happier.

BOOK 2: HOW TO SHRINK YOUR DRAGON

The second book is chock full of ways to shrink your Dragon — figuratively and literally. You'll find out soon why you can't *slay* the Dragon (it has its usefulness), but the name of this game is to get it to relinquish its control over you. If you're being stopped by fear, or worry, then the Dragon is winning. The question becomes: How do you get control back?

Some of the solutions may seem ridiculously simple. You may catch yourself saying, "I just have to do *that? That's it??*" The answer is yes, it's that simple. But simple is not easy, because most often change happens with repetition — and consistency isn't exactly our strong point as humans. You can thank your Dragon for that.

I found it exciting when these tactics started working and was amazed at just how far they reverberated through my life. One new habit or mindset can have a ripple effect that far outreaches where you started. It's exciting.

BOOK 3: STEPPING INTO YOUR GOAT LIFE

The last book is all about identifying and scaling up your GOAT-ness. This is where you'll find lots of habit-changing, life-altering strategies that don't take a lot of time but will take a considerable amount of thought — and action.

Manifestation is a word I'm not happy with, because for some, it means "Sit and wait and the life I want will plop out of the sky." And while I want you to manifest your greatness, it will not arrive on a train for you. You have to *do the work.* You have to make a commitment. I will show you how what we normally say to ourselves that *sounds* like commitment is really your Dragon talking — and how to change that pattern so you get more done, in less time, with way more fun. Happy people do hard work and are wildly successful. Your GOAT work will show you how to find this part of you and live it every day, in every way.

This section will encourage you the most to put the book down and think. Please pause and do that work. The best way to read these books is in small chunks anyway; otherwise, your brain just can't retain the message. When you write down what you're thinking and put words to the dreams, psychologically, it becomes more deeply imprinted on your brain. Throw in talking with someone about what you're doing and what it means to you … and you're almost guaranteed to see huge changes — in yourself and in those around you. Because when you shine more brightly, people will wonder what you're doing and see that you're just "different" in some way they cannot quite put their finger on.

So let's dig in.

First, we start with some factoids about the brain. Not going to lie: I love this stuff because it gives me the rules of the game, and you can only win a game if you know the rules inside and out. Then, we're off to the races.

BOOK 1, PART 1

TIME TO MEET YOUR DRAGON

There's a simple way to understand where your "Dragon" lives. It's in the limbic part of the brain called the amygdala, which is responsible for all sorts of things, like generating emotions and responses to events and people. It is the center of how we see ourselves, too. This tiny almond-shaped ball deep in our brains is small but powerful, and old as dirt.

The amygdala works with the reptilian parts of our brain and brain stem, hence the name "Dragon." "Reptile" just wasn't scary enough. Evolutionarily speaking, this is a very, very old part of our cranium. It developed first, and the newer part of our brain, such as the frontal lobes that generate logic, reasoning, and creativity, came much later. Our Dragon protected our ancestors from saber-tooth tigers, human enemies, and has kept us from falling off cliffs. It also controls our basic functions like breathing, heartbeat, body temperature, and balance.[1] So you can see why this book isn't so much about "slaying" that part of our brains; it's more about shrinking it to its most important functions. The trick is to get our Dragon to work *for* us, not the other way around. And this isn't easy because it's very, very jumpy.

The Dragon has a hair trigger for certain emotions in particular: anger, fear, aggression, and stress. When we become overwhelmed by these emotions, all logic and reasoning flee the scene. And when you add in a threat to our sense of belonging and fitting in, our ability to function becomes almost impossible. We enter a state of panic and reflexive reactions, causing damage to ourselves and to those around us. Our personal emotions and fears concoct scary scenarios of what might come to pass, causing us to throttle back our energy. The sense of belonging drives behaviors that negate the individual in favor of the "greater tribe." We will

---

1   www.thebrain.mcgill.ca

do anything to stay connected — even if it means we hurt ourselves in the process, and we are almost always the victim. We settle, compromise, and avoid asking for what we want — all in the name of conformity and acceptance.

Our Dragon is also responsible for keeping us "safe," and by that, I mean "in the familiar." If you get into a habit of always sleeping in, or staying up late, or eating poorly, or having bad time management habits, your Dragon will want you to keep at it, not because these habits and routines are *good* for you — simply because they are familiar. You've built solid neural pathways for these actions, and your Dragon wants it to stay that way. Anything that threatens these pathways, even if it improves your life, is the equivalent of a death threat. Your Dragon then kicks in and presents myriad reasons as to why fixing that problem is a bad idea. And most often, we give in.

This drive to belong can make you worry constantly about what other people think of you, and where you stand in the pecking order of mate, success, income-earning potential, and status. Where you stand in society means you're either accepted into the tribe and your status is assured, or figuring out how to avoid getting kicked out, shamed, and having to fend off starvation on your own. If truly threatened, we have the capacity to take others down in order to assure ourselves of our place.

The Dragon has a hair trigger for threats to our status and place in life, and loves revenge but only if there's no big fight. Revenge from afar is good. Social media is basically the Dragon's tool, with the emergence of millions of armchair warriors and online bullies who destroy their targets with cruelty, shame, and worse. There's no way we'd say those things in front of our target, but being removed through technology has engendered a bravado for the Dragon-led masses.

While wild animals hunt, look out for danger, eat, mate and repeat because all they have is this lizard brain, we have evolved differently. We started out as pure hunters, running primarily on instinct, but over time, our brains have added new pieces, and those pieces have helped us adapt and grow into the dominant species, one that is rational, creative, curious, and innovative. If evolution isn't your jam, imagine that whatever being created us set us up differently than other species. No matter how you like to look at how we as humans came to be, it's still magical. So, while our Dragon has helped us survive and thrive, it can also be our downfall, keeping us from doing things that advance us in life, business, relationships, the community, and more. And the more we understand how and why this Dragon works, the better chance we have to overcome its impulses.

The most common ways we are puppets to our Dragon are:

- **Fight**: Facing any perceived threat aggressively. Your Dragon likes to talk the big talk but rarely wants to actually fight. There's too much danger of injury.
- **Flight**: Running away from the danger. This is the Dragon's preferred solution. Just do something else — anything!
- **Freeze**: Unable to move or act against a threat. Play dead. The danger will leave (hopefully). No thoughts occur in freeze mode. Your brain goes blank.
- **Fawn**: Immediately acting to try to please to avoid any conflict.[2] This is the belonging urge. Fit in. Don't stand out. Conform. Do what everyone else is doing.

Our response is directly tied to two things:

1. Our perception of the event
2. The belief in our ability to cope with it

If the stress of a situation outstrips the belief in our ability to cope with it, well, away we go! Panic! Threat! Dragons! Oh my!

If you're taking an exam for school, and you're already getting a 98% in the class, your stress level will be relatively low. You know you've got this! If, however, you're scraping by with a 51%, the brain sees the exam as the equivalent of being eaten alive by an evil honey badger that hasn't had a solid meal in over a month.

What happens here is extremely important to recognize. If your brain decides that the event is too much for it to handle, the Dragon leaps into action and slams the door to your frontal lobes — that "thinking" part of the brain that includes reason, rationality, and logic, and retains all the stuff you learned in class. You instantly forget all the stuff you *should know* to answer the questions. You draw a blank, blame the teacher, answer "C" to every question, cry, scream, or just admit you're an idiot and blame it all on your incompetence. This is called an "amygdala hijack" and it's not pretty.

I first read of this phenomenon in Daniel Goleman's 1995 book, *Emotional Intelligence: Why It Can Matter More Than IQ.* In a hijack situation, your ability to find any sort of rational solution is impaired, and you're left with sweaty palms, a racing heart, a tight throat, and an insatiable desire to flee or punch someone out.

Later in this book, I'll show you how to live through one of these hijacks, and even better, how to avoid them altogether. Because every amygdala hijack is a win for the Dragon, yet again.

This process repeats itself several times a day, every day unless you learn to tame it. You can't stop it, because the Dragon is simply too fast, but you *can* control it, and that's where we're going to go from here. No one should be held hostage by emotions, amygdala hijacks, and the fallout from not being our best selves.

HOW YOUR DRAGON WINS

There are countless ways your Dragon wins over your GOAT. What follows is by no means an exhaustive list of ways the Dragon prevents us from becoming the happiest, most content, wealthiest, and fulfilled humans, but it's a great start. If you know how and when your Dragon will strike, you can begin to prepare in advance, preventing the seemingly inevitable hijack, cut off from reason and critical thinking.

WHEN THE "WE ONLY USE 10% OF OUR BRAIN" MYTH IS TRUE

As we have seen, an amygdala hijack occurs when our emotions get way out of whack, causing the Dragon to sense a massive threat and shutting down the connections to the "thinking brain," where the answer to, "*What do I do now?*" resides.

As I said before, the four main emotions that are particularly powerful in triggering a hijack are:

- Anger
- Fear
- Stress
- Aggression

These four create such an imbalance between how we feel and what we do that we can inadvertently destroy businesses, relationships, even ourselves. They are the root of feeling over-whelmed and burned out. Brené Brown describes the feeling of being overwhelmed in *Atlas of the Heart* as "On a scale of 1 to 10, I'm feeling my emotions at about a 10, I'm paying attention to them at about a 5, and understanding them at about a 2." The more time we spend being overwhelmed and emotionally dysfunctional, the more we wreak havoc on every aspect of our lives, minds, and bodies.

When we get inundated by emotions and aren't sure how to deal with them, we start to create narratives in our heads — thoughts of resentment, bitterness, self-sabotage, and hurt. And when we repeat these stories often enough, they become our beliefs. From there, because the beliefs cause us pain, we start spewing our poison onto others, typically those who love us and therefore will be hurt the most. The more someone else hurts, we are falsely told by the Dragon, the better we will feel because surely our pain will transfer to them like an evil Care Bear Stare. Sadly, this is never the case. We keep our pain, but now they have some of it too. For a split second, when we first let fly our poison darts, we feel amazing. But after that incredibly short victory, we fall deeper into the vortex of self-hatred, guilt, and shame. We want to be rid of the pain, but it just won't go away.

Brené Brown details what I have come to call the "shame blame game" in her book *Daring Greatly*. We do not like to feel guilt or shame, because they mean that we've done something wrong, and our Dragon hates to be wrong. So instead of dealing with it or sorting through the feelings to see what's really going on, we blame someone else for it, shifting the pain away from us and squarely on some-one else's shoulders.

I have been guilty of this "shame blame game" many times, but none more poignantly than when it played out on the same day, I read Dr. Brown's descrip-tion in her book.

My husband and I had just bought a condo that we were going to rent out at a resort not far from our home. It was a high-end resort and not a cheap condo, so we wanted to be sure that the tenants we rented it to wouldn't destroy the place or turn into asshole squatters. I do a lot of work with Realtors and have a trea-sure-trove of nightmare stories. I did not want to be one of them!

On the day we were to meet our potential renters, a lovely couple from Quebec and PEI, there was still much to do. They would be arriving at 10:00 am, and I had woken up at 8:30 am, still working off some delicious wine from the night before. I was extremely stressed about meeting these people, having grown up under so much criticism from folks from the church on my ability to create an acceptable home. From not making my pasta sauce from scratch to not having the right tablecloth, the criticisms of times past were rolling through my brain, ratcheting up my already-high anxiety.

There were still boxes to unpack, things to wash and put away, and I was worried I wouldn't get it all done in time. Worse, I was terrified that what I had created in this condo wouldn't be enough, and they'd look at the furnishings with disdain. I was afraid I wouldn't look like a "good" landlord (whatever that meant). I fretted that we wouldn't have everything they needed in our "fully stocked" condo.

I found a thousand things to stress about, so when Marc walked through the kitchen at 9:30 am, saying he was off to shower, I lost my nut. It is with massive regret that I look back on that five-minute tirade, as he stood there, saying nothing. When I was done, he simply continued on his way to the shower, and I fumed and muttered expletives as I finished the work to be done. At 10:00 am, the tenants arrived. Everything was done and put away. They were lovely. We chatted happily for about thirty minutes, and they agreed to rent with us. Mission accomplished! I was still pissed at Marc, who wisely went about his business. He knows me well enough to leave me alone (especially if I'm being quiet. It's a blessing.). I sat down to read Brown's book and opened literally to the page that explained what I had just done: blaming Marc for my own insecurity about tenants, my past pain of criticism and judgment, and my anger at myself for drinking that much wine and sleeping in.

In the moment, full of insecurity, taking ownership of all that pain was too much, and it overwhelmed my system. And so out it all came in a rush of mean words I didn't want to say, knowing that, as they cascaded from my mouth, I was really the one at fault and should really shut up. But when you're in full amygdala hijack mode, there is no mechanism to shut off the valve, and so the poison keeps pouring out.

Later that day, I sheepishly explained to Marc what had happened and apologized profusely for making him the target of my anger and anxiety. Those powerhouse emotions took over my brain and just ran with whatever came to mind. I was not letting the frontal lobes, where rationality, ideas, and solutions reside, to come to my rescue. The connection was lost in the hijack, and my Dragon laughed and laughed and laughed.

Sadly, I've done this since, but each time I catch myself a little earlier, and Marc, as the gentlest and most understanding human on Earth, continues to quietly and kindly remind me that he doesn't need to be my receptacle of pain. I am grateful to have him.

Our limbic system (we can call it the Dragon's lair) is where strong emotions create the most lasting, and often the most painful, memories. We don't remember all the little things that happen in our days. We don't have the brainpower for all of that. But when we have strong emotions, they are burned into our memories to be reused and recycled over and over again. And while there are positive memories and emotions, we are not wired to feel or think of them first. Our past traumas can do us harm over and over as new experiences act as reminders of troubled times past.

It seems like an evolutionary misfire to have our memories created in the same place as our emotions, considering we're already wired to see the bad side of things. But this is what we have, and the Dragon knows how to use it expertly. The more powerfully you react to the world, both positively and negatively, the more memories you will have to dip into as new experiences crop up. Your Dragon will be waiting, so tread carefully.

Looking back on these times, and many, MANY more since, I've realized something: the so-called "myth" that we use only 10% of our brains is, in fact, often true. When we get freaked out and lose all belief in our ability to cope with a situation (or life), the Dragon closes the door to our "thinking" brain. And our "thinking" brain accounts for 90% of its total mass. Hence, when the Dragon wins, we're operating on 10% brainpower.

You can imagine that if you cultivate a way of living constantly in fear, worried that the world will throw something at you that you can't deal with, your Dragon gets stronger and stronger. And, to make matters worse, the longer you stress yourself out, the BIGGER your amygdala gets, physically. The bigger your amygdala, the more it controls your behaviors and emotions, and the more stressed out your nervous system gets. You end up operating at only 10% brain capacity nearly every day.

And that, my friends, leaves us struggling to make our way through life. The Dragon is lightning-fast, and in a battle between it and the "thinking" brain, it will win 100% of the time. No contest. It may seem like a hopeless task to shut our Dragon down when it's so old, so fast, and so powerful. But your GOAT is the answer, if only you'd give it more of your attention.

Right now, it's important to become aware of all the ways your Dragon can win, so get your notebooks ready: you'll want to take stock of the ways it's gaining the upper hand in your life, so you can apply the appropriate strategy to shrink it down.

TESTS, FEAR, AND BRAIN FREEZE

I hated tests. Still do. I haven't taken a single test since college. No matter what the test was about, even if I was doing well in class, as soon as I sat down, I felt like I was going to completely forget what I'd learned and then fail. My brain draws an immediate and complete blank. The same happened when I was called on in class. I feel the same way when a police car drives up behind me. I'm instantly packing heat, have stashed one pound of cocaine in my glove box beside the loaded gun, and I have a kidnap victim in my trunk who's bleeding from the stab wound I gave him. It's immediate sweat and panic. I know it's insanity, but my body isn't getting that calming message. I'm in full amygdala hijack, and it won't let go.

I hated tests and exams viscerally because no matter what my grade was going in, I approached every test as if it were going to eat me alive. I'd never been great at memorization, so I created acronyms for acronyms, terrified that I'd draw a complete blank upon turning over the paper.

I remember writing my third-year finance midterm. There were seven questions. I was in a room with 300 people in a huge lecture hall, writing on the world's smallest desk, balancing my pens, calculator, and my self-worth on my lap.

As the exam bell rang to begin, I read question one, and totally blanked. So, I flipped to page two. Surely, I'd know how to answer that one … nope. On and on I went, turning the papers over, until I had read every single question, having absolutely *no* clue how to answer any of them. I flipped the exam back to the first question and stared at the mint-green paper for five minutes, wondering whether a lifetime career as a Walmart greeter was more likely than a career in business.

With a deep breath, I started writing whatever came to mind. I eventually tortured my way through the exam, taking the entire three hours and whatever extra few minutes I was able to squeeze out as the professor came and collected the tests from the other stragglers. I handed it in, not looking up, packed up my things, and trudged out of the hall.

I shuffled to the elevator, thinking of the McDonalds drive-thru jobs I'd be applying for. Just as the doors were closing, my finance prof steps in. Ohno-honoohno. He was the most intimidating person I'd ever met. Tall, white flowing hair (it was distractingly gorgeous), Israeli-born, slight accent, and a devastating way of picking you out of the crowd to ask if you had any clue what he was talking about. (He'd say, "You, in the red hat, blue sweater, looking through your bag to avoid answering this question." There was no hiding.)

I was terrified every single class that he'd call on me. When a girl in the class couldn't answer a simple accounting question, he dragged her down to the front after class, gave her a Spanish Inquisition-style interrogation as to why she was unable to answer the simplest accounting question, and then dragged her to the accounting department and yelled at *them* for doing such a bad job in teaching us accounting, so how was *he* supposed to teach us finance!?

All of these memories shot through my body like an electric shock, and I was sure he was going to ask me what I got on question 3. I started sweating all over again. As you can see, this is my body's stress response: really aromatic and squishy. I think the elevator slowed down to a crawl. It was taking forever, and it was getting harder and harder to avoid eye contact. Oh no. He was going to talk to me.

"How did you do?" he asked kindly.

I think I said something super witty like, "I don't think I failed," and mentally urged the elevator to hurry UP! It didn't, and I died a little inside. I might even have peed a little. When those elevator doors opened, I literally ran. Turns out I got a B+ (which was better than the D+ I got in finance the year before). My Dragon had had a stranglehold on my brain on that exam, but I fought it enough to squeak out a few thoughts. But the pain I endured, unnecessarily, scarred me for life.

Since graduating in 1999, the only test I've taken was to get my motorcycle license. The fear of not having answers to questions of any kind, no matter the situation, haunts me still. When asked to show the motorcycle instructor where the high beams were on my test, I temporarily forgot what "high beams" were, let alone where the button was. Sometimes I wonder what else I could have done in life if I didn't have this fear. Would I have gone back to school to get my MBA? Would I have gotten certifications and enhanced my education and skill sets? Would it have mattered? I'll never know.

OUR (DIS)COMFORT ZONE – "FAMILIAR" IS NOT ALWAYS "GOOD"

One of the ways our Dragon loves to control us is by creating the "comfort zone" myth. I've never understood the term because anyone who lives firmly in this zone is mostly miserable, afraid, unfulfilled, and unsuccessful. They often think they should be further along than they are, and it makes them feel even more inadequate. It is not comfortable; it's familiar, and those are two very different things.

Steven is one of my favorite people in the entire world. He's this big, burly, well-dressed gay man from Kansas with a smile that makes his eyes disappear. You always know when he's happy: you can't see his eyeballs anymore. I love that smile.

When we first started working together, I didn't see that smile very often. He had had a lot of problems relating to and dealing with his family and community. It's not easy being gay in a small town. There was hurt layered on hurt, and in some of our calls, I'd sit quietly as the tears rolled down his bearded cheeks. It broke my heart.

He had been trying his entire life to live in his comfort zone of not really saying anything, of keeping the peace, getting along. He made himself small because he was afraid people wouldn't accept all of him. He hoped that by doing so, there might be less conflict, but it never seemed to work, certainly not for him. This would soon change, but the fear of taking on family and his reputation in his community was a massive undertaking.

Once he really stepped up for himself, there would be no turning back. I've had a number of clients who took deep breaths and stepped forward for themselves, sometimes just speaking up, sometimes starting life 2.0 in a new career. Each time, it was gut-wrenchingly scary. Their initial excitement and bravery takes them past some of their Dragon's fear barriers until that honey-moon phase ends, and they stand there, bedazzled by the light of the reality they now face. Their Dragons then have a field day, imagining how conversations could go wrong, or depressing them by comparing them to these industry titans they are now up against. They begin to retreat back to what is comfortable and familiar — giving up on standing up for themselves or going back to get jobs instead of launching a company or diverting their attention away from the hard work ahead. They begin to fill their time with endless time-wasters — taking classes to fill up the days, playing video games, walking the dog, folding laundry, or cleaning their office (again).

Our brains like things to feel the same, and whenever you do something brand new, your Dragon will start to magnify the emotions you have about *other* things. I had an entire team that I sent on a two-week individualized plan to become more self-sufficient at growing their businesses, instead of relying on the team lead to do it for them. At the end of the two weeks, 100% of them did not live up to their own commitments. For some, "other work" suddenly became "so important" to do, instead of the work that would truly impact their lives. That work and those distractions had always been there, but *now it had to be done first!* The "familiar" work, though clearly wasting time, felt more comfortable. The excuses kept rolling in — they suck at time management, family things came up, they slept in. In moments of bravery — especially when making a life-changing transformation — your Dragon brings out all of its weapons. "*Get back! Get back!*" it cries. And it usually works.

Comfort zones may seem comfortable, but they are NOT safe. They are simply familiar. Your Dragon doesn't care if "familiar" is "good"; it just wants predictability. This is how people stay in relationships that are unhealthy or even dangerous. It's also why they keep finding the same type of horrid person over and over. They're familiar, not good, but something we've seen before. Your brain will always take the path of least resistance.

So, what may look like a healthy situation or relationship to you will look unreachable for someone used to being in an abusive or oppressive situation. They can't see themselves with a better person. They have no context and no frame of reference. And to get that context, it requires hard work and courage, things hard to come by naturally. This is just another tactic the Dragon uses to keep you exactly where you are: making things look so far out of reach or beyond your abilities. *Don't bother. It's not in the cards for you. Stay where you are.*

In the comfort zone, nothing changes. All is "well." Few decisions are made because decisions mean you might have to stick your neck out and defend yourself, and that's dangerous. Instructions only, please. "Just tell me what to do," says your comfort-zone voice. Keep things as they are. Keep things quiet. And yet every time you hold back, you give your power away, making it even less likely to change the trajectory of your life.

Our memories play a huge role in creating the structure of our comfort zones. Robin Sharma's chapter on fear in *The Secret Letters of the Monk Who Sold His Ferrari* has a great quote:

> *"Indeed, the greatest risk in life is taking no risks. But every time we do that which we fear, we take back the power that fear has stolen from us — for on the other side of our fears lives our strength."* [3]

The Dragon hosts memories of your fears and emotionally-charged experiences, and so with every new environment you encounter or any new person you meet, it's attempting to categorize it and "place" it within the emotional realm of what you've already gone through. If something checks out as being familiar and safe, the Dragon encourages you to proceed, even if you might be hurt or even killed in the process. It doesn't see the trap. It doesn't actually care. If something fits within the comfort zone boundaries, it's all systems go.

So instead of being safe, your comfort zone is the most distressing, painful, self-sabotaging place you can be. The longer you stay there, the stronger your Dragon becomes and the harder it is to break out.

BABY BIRD SYNDROME

A lot of the agents at Steven's real estate brokerage suffered badly from what I call "Baby Bird Syndrome." Steven is a powerhouse. He appears to have all the answers — to know what to do — and has developed a fearlessness in getting

---

3   The Secret Letters of the Monk Who Sold His Ferrari, p. 68

things done. He'd been working hard on shrinking his Dragon, and it showed. The rest of the team in his organization trusted his judgment so much that they forgot to trust their own. They just gathered around him, like baby birds, waiting for him to give them instructions.

I started working with Steven when this situation had come to a head and it was driving him nuts. He was working insane hours and was frustrated at the team's lack of initiative and decision-making. They just waited for him. We worked together on how he contributed to this problem by handing the team answers and doing the work his team was more than capable of doing on their own. He'd often get fed up, and just handle the situation with an "Oh screw it, I'll just do it" attitude. In order to cure the baby bird syndrome, he had to stop both feeding the team answers and doing the work for them.

He brought me in to coach the team on how to believe in *themselves* and their *own* abilities to grow their businesses. As independent contractors within a large brokerage, they got perks from having their license there, but were responsible for their own success or failure. Problem was, they were acting more like employees than entrepreneurs, a common theme in the real estate industry.

I'd gathered the data about the team and their behaviors before I arrived to the two-day coaching event, so I had a pretty good idea of what was going on and why they felt so incapable of stepping up. I wanted to see them in action outside a classroom setting first, to see if I was right. I landed the night before the conference and met everyone in the swanky lobby bar. The team had been there a while and was liberally partaking in the fun. Some on the leadership team felt that food should be in order, or the libations might make the next day impossible.

I was standing with Steven and his husband, watching this situation unfold. Two of his team approached, asking what the plans were for dinner. With a wink to me, Steven said, "Whatever you want." In the past, he'd have told them where they'd go for dinner. But he knew I needed him to really practice letting the decisions be made by his team — even if it's just "what to do for dinner."

But his response was met with blank stares. They stood there, unsure of what to do. They asked him again, what did he want? Where should they go? They listed a few options and still stood there, waiting for him to decide for them.

Knowing that he could not just hand them an answer, Steven tried a few more times to get them to make a decision, and they simply would not. I finally said, "Tacos! You want tacos!" Their faces lit up and off they went to find tacos with the team.

This was trouble. Over the course of the next year, I worked with everyone on how to let the Baby Bird Syndrome die. Any time someone from the organization asked a question about what to do, the leadership team was to ask right back, "What do YOU think you should do about it?"

Eventually this question became so irritating to the group that they began to just *do the work*. They made decisions. They did the work that would make a difference to their lives. They worked together and collaborated to find solutions instead of assuming Steven would have the answer. They were liberated! They'd flown the nest.

They took the Dragon off the walls of their castle and built up the ramparts so they were protected from feeling powerless or incapable. Sometimes, they fall *off* those ramparts, but someone throws down a ladder and they climb back up.

Your Dragon will want you to stay safe, avoid decisions, and never make anything your fault. It loves making you a baby bird, but just like your comfort zone, you'll either outgrow the nest and fly — or fade into nothing. Fly, baby, fly.

HOW MAKING A "BIG LEAP" MAKES YOU SICK — AND WHY THAT'S AWESOME

The second year I played beer-league baseball with Marc, he went away for the second game of the season. I'd have to go alone. I'd played the year before and had had an absolute blast, but the idea of going to the game this year without him filled me with terror. I'm what I would call "situationally introverted/extroverted with a splash of performance anxiety." There are events in which I feel completely at ease, doing my thing, chatting up my friends, and having a great time. There are other situations, however, when my guts squeeze, and I want to barf and poop myself at the same time. And that was baseball.

Playing baseball without Marc filled me with dread and panic. Each year, our teammates changed, so I didn't really know many of them. Marc was familiar to me in an unfamiliar setting, and I relied on him (clearly too much). I didn't want to let my team down, but the fear of showing up was crippling me. The stories

I created about how I'd embarrass myself, strike out, fall down, and so on were vivid and awful.

But I figured I knew how to lick this problem and get there, with Marc or not. I'd just finished reading Gay Hendrick's book *The Big Leap,* which detailed what he called the "Upper Limit Problem," which you hit when you do something that exceeds the outer reaches of your comfort zone. And when you get close to moving past that comfort zone point of no return, weird things start to happen.

You get sick. You have an accident. Everything that used to seem unimportant suddenly becomes the most urgent and pressing matter that has to be dealt with immediately (to avoid doing the thing that will drive you past your Upper Limit).

People around you start acting funny; they're meaner than normal or ambush you with some pointless argument you're not expecting. You start picking fights for no reason. You sabotage yourself — you sleep in, fire someone for no reason, or end a long-standing friendship.

Most people see these as "signs" that they should go back and retreat to their safety zones where things are miserable but predictable. They shrink themselves down once again because growth is hard and painful. Truthfully, Hendricks explains that these signals are actually your upper limit *symptoms*, indicators that you're about to make a leap to your genius level where true creativity, fulfillment, and joy reside. All you have to do is push through. Easier said than done, and your Dragon makes it feel impossible.

I tried to be rational about playing ball that Friday. We pitch to our own team, so strikeouts aren't common. It's fun, and the people are nice. No one takes it too seriously, and we all head to the bar after the game to hang out and have even more fun.

As the week crept toward Friday night, I kept telling myself that I'd be perfectly okay. It's just a game. No one cares if I hit or ground out or pick my nose all game long. They're my friends. I like them. I've met them all at least once, and they were not mean. It's totally 100% okay!

But my body had other plans. By Friday morning, I had a temperature of 104°F. I was sick as a dog. The only thing that truly knocks me sideways is a fever, and my Dragon was well aware of this fact. I had to cancel. I could barely lift my head.

I was furious with myself because I *knew* it was going to happen, and no amount of self-persuasion changed a thing. By Saturday, of course, I was miraculously healed.

Nanci, who joined my group coaching program in the spring of 2022, had a similar experience but she went even further. Faced with making seismic adjustments to her life and business, she got *really* sick. She had to have her gall bladder removed and popped a rib in some giant coughing fit. The week following this drama and physical pain, she showed up on our coaching call with a smile and laugh, regaling us on this miserable situation as if it was the best thing that ever happened to her. She pushed through! She'd made it!

Nanci knew it meant she was making a big leap, and it excited the daylights out of her. I was ecstatic for her — not because she went through horrible physical pain, but because she'd powered through. She went on to make giant strides in her business that made me tear up at the end as she described just how far she'd come. If she had let those physical blocks stop her, the outcome would have been vastly different.

Most people never make it like Nanci. As for me, I finally sorted myself out and can play ball without feeling like I'm going to barf or take a nervous poop before I walk out the door. Most folks retreat; they fall back. They see the pain and retract and recoil. And the Dragon wins again.

COMPARISON CULTURE (YOUR INTERNAL CANCEL CULTURE!)

I can't count the number of calls I've had with my high-performing clients where they said, "I'm just not as far along as (that guy/girl/team/business/whatever)." These are people that make seven-figures, have great personal lives, and have teams that want to show up every day for them as their best selves. But they still have a feeling of being "not enough." The question is, not good enough for what — and based on what metrics? How are they measuring their success? It baffled me, so naturally, I went hunting for answers, starting with my own past in dealing with these same comparison reflexes.

When I was running my marketing agency, I'd constantly size myself up against other agencies. If I saw them on the speaker list for a conference, I'd wonder why I wasn't invited. What were they doing — should I do it too? Can

I hit the "Two Comma Club" and get that plaque I see on people's walls? Do I have enough clients to be legit? Every day as I scrolled through my Facebook feed, I'd see my competitors publishing an article (*Do I need a PR person?*) or a book (*Should I write a book?*) or doing any number of things I thought maybe I should be doing too. It was exhausting and made me feel like garbage.

As these feelings of being left behind grew, I'd start imitating someone else, believing that if I did it just like them, I'd achieve the exact same success. Then I'd compare my results to theirs and wonder where I went wrong because no matter how hard I tried, my outcomes were nowhere near what they said they'd achieved. Constantly chasing someone else's results made me feel hopeless, stupid, insecure, and miserable.

Comparison is the biggest creativity, success, and joy killer. It's also instinctive — we can't stop the reflex. Brené Brown describes it as "*The crush of conformity from one side and competition from the other — it's trying to simultaneously fit in and stand out.*"[4] Our compulsion to fit into the "tribe" propels us to look around, size everyone up, and see where we stand. But the narrative to stand out and not conform is equally as loud. We end up stuck in the push-pull of living up to other people's standards, where the rules change like the wind and the goal seems further and further away. We compare everything: our parenting, our spouses, our incomes, our looks, and our values, or lack thereof. We compare religious beliefs, how well our kids play soccer or their marks in school. We compare our car to the one beside us at the stoplight. Sometimes we gloat that we're better off, but more often than not, we're wishing things were different.

Brené continues, "*In general, however, frequent social comparisons are not associated with life satisfaction or the positive emotions of love and joy but are associated with the negative emotions of fear, anger, shame and sadness.*"

Our Dragon knows that we can't help but compare ourselves to others, gauging whether they're doing better or worse than how we perceive our own position in the pecking order. But as Brené makes clear, we feel like crap when we do it, even if we're coming out on top. The more you compare, the worse you feel. Our emotions start getting confusing, with guilt and shame mixing with feeling

---

4   Atlas of the Heart, Brené Brown. p. 26

accomplished and successful. If we don't properly regulate our emotions, then we're doomed to fall into the comparison self-sabotaging disaster zone.

The more time we invest in comparisons, the less time we have to spend on ourselves, growing, expanding, or striving for more happiness and success. If you're not looking at what's ahead of you, you'll miss all the road signs — both the warning signs and the opportunities to live your GOAT life. You cannot drive a car looking at the vehicles in the other lanes. You don't win a race by looking at the people beside you. Our Dragon knows this. With every comparison that we don't control, it gets bigger and bigger, voicing its lies in our ears. We believe more and more of these false stories to be true. This in turn drives us to feel like the lives of "others" are so much better, and so far out of reach that there's no point in even trying.

We fall back to just surviving. Punching in and out. Doing what we have to. Hating Mondays and always looking for Friday's relief and release from the humdrum of work. We then go home to a ho-hum life that doesn't thrill us; it has its own sense of emptiness. So, we go out for beers with neighbors or friends and spend the night comparing ourselves to them — their jobs, looks, spouses, clothes, and so on — and the whole nastiness continues its vicious cycle. Even if this story was about someone who was successful by industry standards, if they spend their time worrying about what everyone else is doing, they won't be on top for long.

Robin Sharma has a wonderful way of describing our tendency to imitate and pretend: *"constructing some plastic life that society had convinced them to inhabit."* [5]

The plastic life is not the real one that you should be living. It's blank, empty, and lifeless. You strive to live someone else's life, or run someone else's business, rather than focusing on the things that light you up and set your passions on fire. You're a clone, not a king or queen. You're just like everyone else, and your value loses its meaning, particularly to you. And if you can't see what *you* bring to the table, and what makes you amazing, the possibility of living a life you're proud of goes up in flames.

The Dragon wins every time we take to heart that we are "lesser than" or "falling behind." It wins when we give up on trying because what other people are

---

5   The Secret Letters of the Monk Who Sold His Ferrari p. 58

doing just seems "too hard" or "easy for them, but not for me." Everything you want is up to you; it just depends on whether you're looking at what's in front of you or not.

PROCRASTINATION, AVOIDANCE, AND INCONSISTENCY

Procrastination, inconsistency, and flat out avoiding the work my clients should be doing rank #1 in the list of bad habits. As soon as I push them to do something different, a thousand excuses cascade from their mouths. They try to convince me that doing laundry in the middle of the day is as important as getting new clients, but it doesn't fly. One of my favorite questions to ask is, "What did you do *instead* of the work you were *supposed* to be doing?"

The answers can be both depressing and hilarious. Here are some of their top responses:

➤ *I did the laundry* (top response, believe it or not, especially if they work from home).
➤ *I walked the dog (five times ... in one day).*
➤ *I cleaned my kitchen (top response)/desk/whatever.*
➤ *I played video games.*
➤ *I went to the beach.*
➤ *I took someone to an appointment.*
➤ *I thought about it a lot.*
➤ *I messed around with my computer/tech.*
➤ *I went for coffee (with someone unrelated to business to fill time).*
➤ *I went for a three-hour lunch (again, not to build business but to fill time).*
➤ *I took a class (on something they'd never use).*
➤ *I participated in a "mastermind" or discussion group (after which they've never done a thing).*
➤ *I had to wait for the (household appliance) to be installed.*

The list is extensive, but you get the point.

In *The War of Art* by Steven Pressfield, he talks about how our Dragon (he calls it "our resistance") has a counterpart: *rationalization*. If we just avoid work, we feel guilt and shame. That doesn't feel good; our Dragon knows that if we felt guilt and shame, we'd look to avoid those feelings and start doing unfamiliar things.

Enter rationalization. Instead of guilt and shame, our Dragon presents us with the spin doctor's reasonable justification for putting things off. Unfortunately, many of these rationalizations are true. An uncle may legitimately need to get to the doctor and can't drive. Our dog legitimately needs to go for a walk. The house is truly cluttered. We'll lose the extra coins or points from our game unless we play it today for at least an hour (or two) at precisely 2 pm. There are a ton of reasons I can come up with to avoid writing this book, making calls, or prepping for an upcoming conference.

But all of this, Pressfield shows us, means jack-bo-diddly. Tolstoy had thirteen kids and still managed to write *War and Peace.* Elon Musk has seven kids (maybe more?) and runs Tesla, SpaceX, and manages a host of other investments. In Ashlee Vance's biography of Elon Musk, Musk explains that if he doesn't think you're doing your job well enough, or if he gives you a problem and you don't think you can solve it, he'll give you about two weeks to figure it out. If you haven't solved the problem, he'll fire you and do it himself. Russia wouldn't give him the rockets he needed for SpaceX, so on the plane home, he figured out how to do it himself at a fraction of the cost.

Seth Godin has written tomes about how people will do amazing work but then never "ship" (deliver, execute, finish the job, take it to market). You can almost hear his frustration in *Linchpin* and *The Practice*, urging readers to do something — anything! People endlessly fiddle with their work and rationalize away actually putting it out there. They call themselves "perfectionists" because it sounds better than the truth, which is, "I'm scared witless to launch."

I've had clients for whom I had to pause their coaching programs because week after week, they came with excuses instead of achievements. The excuses sounded 100% legit: taking family members to appointments, helping another colleague out on something they were working on, or mentoring a newbie because it made them feel wanted and smart. They walked the dog (again). They cleaned the house (again). Rearranged furniture. Went to Costco (all day???). I wanted to pull my hair out. It's the blight of being a coach: I can counsel, consult, encourage, and motivate, but I cannot get people off their asses.

No matter the excuse, my clients eventually fessed up about why they were wasting thousands of dollars paying me to listen to them rationalize their inaction. They dreaded our calls. They'd try to cancel to avoid me entirely. They would do anything to prevent themselves from feeling guilty about stalling out. That brief moment when they felt great having made a decision to not do the work quickly evaporated, replaced with the dread of our call, knowing my first question is always, "So, how'd it go this week with (work they were supposed to do)?"

But they only felt really bad for about three seconds because hot on the heels of the guilt and shame came the Dragon's spin doctor to make them feel like, in that "not going to do it" decision-making moment, they could "give" the responsibility of the work to some-one else. It wasn't up to them. It wasn't their fault. They can't help it … And so, they do whatever comes to mind *other* than the work they *should* be doing.

Sadly, that "not my fault so it's okay" feeling dissipates almost as quickly as it arrives, and once again, we feel bad that we're not progressing, not happy, not successful, or just "not there yet." It can make our goals and desires seem so far away and more unattainable than ever. But the fear of taking responsibility and moving past the feelings of dread, failure, rejection, judgment (that list can be *very* long) prevents us from getting past the inconsistency and excuses. And the Dragon wins another round.

Fear magnifies everything, making it seem so much harder than it actually is. Making a phone call is physically simple — the fear of what someone will say is what stops us. Having a tough conversation is not really hard when you know what to say, but the fear of how the other person will react keeps us settling with "It'll be okay someday …" And the Dragon is the one holding the magnifying glass, showing you the dangers and many possible disastrous outcomes, ensuring that you see things precisely as it wants you to, so you'll stay "safe," do nothing, and hold the line.

MAKING EXCUSES AND AVOIDING DISAPPOINTMENT

Excuses go hand in hand with procrastination, but they are so potent and evil that they deserve their own section in this book. I shot a video once called "How big is your 'but'?" YouTube didn't appreciate the reference and took it down (clearly their AI doesn't get the double-entendre). But the message was simple:

The more you make the same excuse, the bigger the "but" you'll have, causing you to re-use the same excuse over and over again until it feels like a legitimate reason to avoid the work you're supposed to be doing.

If you tell yourself a story enough times, your brain believes it to be the truth, regardless of how ridiculous it really is. In my world as a high-performance coach, I hear tons of excuses as to why my clients aren't ready to work with me (or any coach, for that matter). They think they are disadvantaged somehow. They lack opportunity. Society is not built for them. They don't have the ideas. They can't do this on their own (and they go get a business partner that contributes nothing but makes them feel safe). They don't have time. They don't have the money. They don't believe they'd do the work. They have a puppy. They have kids. They have no kids. It's not hard to find excuses. It's the easiest thing in the world, which is why as humans we are so good at it.

When I was getting my high-performance coaching certification, Brendan Burchard put up a slide I have used in nearly all my workshops ever since. In his studies on what makes people high performers, he discovered that there are attributes and traits that have zero correlation to someone's ability to make more money, have stronger relationships, and feel successful and fulfilled. Here's the list of things that have *nothing* to do with your ability to live your GOAT life:

- Age
- Gender
- Nationality
- Intelligence
- Personality
- Strengths
- Creativity
- Empathy
- Years of experience
- Compensation

I've talked with people who feel "too old" to start a new chapter of their lives and instead decide to keep punching the clock and mailing it in, even though it makes them absolutely miserable. I've tried to convince women that they don't need a male business partner to be successful and credible. I've managed to convince some that their years of experience (or lack thereof) can be their greatest asset.

I've coached many a client who never finished college, drilling into them the need to ignore whatever has been said about the connection between education and success. Instead, their focus must be 100% on living and working using their incredible talents and skills. My mentor, Frank Kern, dropped out of college to pursue his own thing. As of 2020, according to The Google, his net worth is $35 million. Not too shabby (he's funny and the most helpful, down-to-earth multi-millionaire I know).

Our excuses make us feel justified about not taking steps beyond our current situation. We almost feel proud of our reasons to hold back. That is, until we look around and start noticing our colleagues passing us by or people stop calling to ask for an opinion. But if you're a master excuse-maker, you'll find a way to rationalize and convince yourself that there is no way you'd be able to achieve (insert awesome life-changer here). Not a chance. They're going to fail, just you wait.

You tell yourself that it's best not to start because what if you don't achieve what you set out to do? You can't handle the disappointment, your Dragon says. Then it will be far worse (or so you say to yourself at night when your thoughts start swirling and that niggling idea of "*What if…?*" starts clawing at your insides).

Disappointment is one of the toughest emotions to process and from which to recover. Our desire to avoid this feeling can feel so powerfully dangerous that sometimes we do what I call "striking first," where we kill any hope of the desired outcome so it's literally impossible to be disappointed or hurt. I've coached some people through relationship challenges where they had adopted the habit of hurting the other person first, so if their partner said anything unkind, they felt it was okay because they'd struck first. I know people who planned to set out to door-knock to meet people in their neighborhood, only to wait until it's too dark … so it's not safe anymore. Back inside they go. Instead of having a tough conversation that might resolve distressing issues, they verbally punched and smacked away, all to justify themselves if they were hurt in return, or if someone slammed a door in their face.

To avoid disappointment is to doom yourself to it. Worse, it can morph into regret; and by the time you hit regret, it's likely too late to rectify things. Your Dragon loves regret. It wants you to bathe in regret, wallow in it, feel stuck in it. Disappointment is just its precursor, and since your Dragon thinks these are terrible feelings, it encourages you to avoid anything that might not work out as planned or that might generate criticism you can't take.

And god help you if you disappoint those you look up to. Sometimes we can deal with not living up to our own standards, but if we imagine our parents, colleagues, mentors, or bosses looking at us with *that look* — we cringe physically and emotionally. Humans love external validation, but it's a cruel master. We never know when we'll get it, because we aren't in other peoples' heads. So now you combine powerful validation from those you look up to with its inconsistent delivery, and you're even more doomed to constantly strive to live up to standards that shift and move like the sands of the desert.

Your Dragon fills your mental bathtub with these emotions and fears, and lulls you into believing that you truly are safer there, instead of trying anything that might disappoint you, or those you look up to. Except one day, your Dragon might just push you under, and then what are you left with?

PAIN IDENTITIES: FROZEN IN TIME

At some point, our excuses and stories start to become a part of us. We begin to associate ourselves with our pain, trauma, and experiences. These identities become particularly dangerous when they prevent us from moving forward with our lives, careers, or businesses. We start to build walls to protect these fairy tales and get vicious if something challenges them and their perceived truth.

On Wednesdays growing up, us kids would go to our church for a youth program. What I remember most was that the final thirty minutes of the evening was dedicated to reciting scripture from memory. My older sister has a mind like a trap — she'd read a passage and remember it for days. I'd have to read and reread even the smallest passage to commit it to memory, only to have it disappear from my brain when my name was called. Awards or prizes were given out each week, and as my sister earned a growing collection, my shelves remained bare. I was seven years old, but from that defining moment, I convinced myself that I had a horrible memory.

This became my identity. I reminded myself of it constantly before every test or exam and ahead of every meeting at work or presentation I had to make when I started my own business.

"This is who I am," I would declare defiantly and angrily, "and I always will be." I felt hopeless in changing it, so I decided that acquiescing to this identity would hurt less.

According to Carol Dweck in *Minsdset,* this is a classic "fixed mindset." We believe that our traits, behaviors, talents, and even our futures are so set in stone as to be completely unchangeable. Here's how it plays out for someone with a fixed mindset (nod if this sounds like you).

A fixed mindset person believes that intelligence is static, which leads to ...

- Avoiding challenges
- Giving up easily
- Seeing effort as fruitless or worse
- Ignoring helpful feedback, particularly negative feedback
- And ultimately feeling threatened by the success of others

This is how the anger sets in. We become angry with ourselves for not being able to change this part of us. Instead of figuring out how to get around it, we slump further into the despair. As a result, we plateau early, settling into a way of life that is a small version of what we are capable of, never quite achieving success or happiness, and then being bitter and resentful of those who do. We blame our limitations and use them as excuses, rationalizing away our inaction. The cycle continues endlessly, picking up new pain identities and excuses, new suffering, and more anger.

Pain — emotional, mental, and physical — plays a massively important role in defining who we believe we are and how we show up in the world. Our fixed mindsets show up everywhere. At sixteen, I hurt my knee. My doctor gave me a few exercises, but they were a pain in the ass, and I'd always forget to do them. For thirty years, I favored that knee. It hurt when I drove, sat on planes, or at the movie theater. I couldn't walk down stairs properly. I'd hop up and down the stairs, leaning on my left leg for support. I couldn't do things like hike or ride my motorcycle without pain. Then one lovely day, Denzil, my athletic trainer, told me what was really going on — as a teen, my kneecap just grew a little wonky. Totally fixable. I wanted to scream! I'd spent thirty years hobbling around, convinced that I'd just have to live with this pain when all along, *it was totally fixable?!?* I'm happy to say I'm bouncing all over the place, albeit carefully. It's not 100%, but I can do a mean squat on the racks now without falling over!

Like with my knee and my supposedly bad memory, we absorb these stories, real or fictitious, and our actions wrap around these beliefs. Our emotions run high when our identities are challenged, and we become angry and defensive. We often don't know who we are without our pain, our victimhood, and our supposed deficiencies. You've probably come across people who are so entrenched in this victimhood, they can't let it go. If they're not a victim, who are they? If they're not a perfectionist, how do they behave? Since they've never lived these other identities, they hold back, unsure of how to change their programming.

The more the pain is "ours," the harder it will be to release it. And while it is impossible to release all our fixed mindsets, your Dragon will fiercely defend the ones that are most risky, that might make you look stupid or weak in front of others, or make mistakes that could cause loss or pain.

For years, I sat back, thinking I'd be a great "wing man" but never smart enough to run my own business. I decided I would never be able to go on great hikes because my knee was shot. I had a bad memory, so I never took another test after college. I wasn't smart enough. And these are just the tip of the iceberg of the limitations I'd imposed on myself. My Dragon was gigantic, with scales like armor and a fire that burned up all hope for me to be happy and successful.

The longer we identify with our pain, our trauma, or our fears, the stronger our Dragon gets and becomes harder to beat down. Our cumulative experiences are how we got to where we are today. To challenge our mindsets about those traumas, big and small, and how they contribute to how we see and act *today*, is to begin to grow and flourish. The objective is never to push our pasts away or let all our stories go and pretend nothing happened. But rather it's to stop the association repeatedly being made that we are who we are and cannot change, that we are relegated to a mediocre version of ourselves. Your Dragon loves to make you feel that what others have, how they live, work, and love, is just "not for you." It's all lies, but the more staunchly you hold your pain identities, the more you believe them to be true.

PERVASIVE UNHAPPINESS

"Crippling unhappiness." That's how I described my life back in 2017. I'd built my marketing agency into a powerhouse, with a team of fourteen spread across the world and a steady stream of clients and international speaking gigs. Having put my life together after the crash, I now had an amazing husband. Beautiful children. Good friends. But every day, I woke up feeling miserable, like a black cloud was sitting heavily on my chest. I hated every day. I hated every email that came in. Everything was just hard, unfulfilling, and gave me nothing but heartburn and sleepless nights. I worked ninety hours a week, and I was burning out.

I was suffering from "pervasive unhappiness," a misery that appears everywhere — in your relationships, your business, your first thoughts upon waking, and as you toss and turn in the middle of the night, unable to sleep. It invades your thoughts and slows your progress. It causes you to completely miss opportunities. There's a nifty process in our brains called "reticular activation," which is basically our internal algorithm. Whatever we tell our brains to look for, that's what it sees. Our brains have two main systems for processing information: System 1 (which I call our Internal Google), which processes tens of millions of bits of data per second. We don't really remember all this stuff, but we're sensing it. Then, there's System 2, which is the slower part where we think, mull things over, and make decisions. I call this our Search Bar.

When we enter words, phrases, or questions onto this Search Bar, our Internal Google will bring up results based on what we've seen and felt before and present it back to us as how we perceive the world. The more miserable you are, and the more you tell yourself how miserable you are, the more you see the world as miserable too. If you tell yourself, "That's not possible" or "I can't afford that," or "I don't deserve that," your brain will present all the appropriate proof. It's all you will see so it will feel true. But you're simply not getting all the results — just the ones your algorithm has determined to be most popular and familiar. The more pervasive and frequent our bouts of unhappiness, the more we train our brain systems to make these results permanent. We begin to see recurring proof that our lives are unhappy and unfulfilling because our world literally feels like it's confirming what we think. And the cycle whirls away, blinding us further to opportunities to stop the death spiral of misery. In *The War of Art*, Pressfield explains the way it feels like this:

> "We're bored, we're restless. We can't get no satisfaction. There's guilt but we can't put our finger on the source. We want to go back to bed; we want to get up and party. We feel unloved and unlovable. We're disgusted. We hate our lives. We hate ourselves." [6]

Unhappy people do not do the hard work. They may appear successful, but they're just miserable inside. My father ran a $4B steel company and would host parties at our home. I can count on one hand the people who actually looked happy and content, and these were the scions of the business community, the "most successful," the ones you read about in the paper. But their lives were empty, their marriages often a sham, and all the planes and cars in the world would never make them feel satisfied.

Back in my agency days, I think I woke up feeling wretched every morning. But one day, it no longer made sense to me because if I was honest, I had a lot of good things going on. The decision to try to reprogram my Internal Google was daunting, but it worked. There's a lot more on this later in this book, so have no fear: your algorithm is in for a massive adjustment!

Your Dragon will always be on hand to whisper reminders of your deficiencies, and will make them look insurmountable. It would rather you be safe and miserable than happy and taking risks. Unhappiness is a terrible feeling, and Dragons keep you there because if you were happy, you'd start doing hard work.

---

6   The War of Art, Steven Pressfield. p. 31

THE UNDOING PROCESS

To look back on an event that ended badly, and say, "*If only …,*" seeking ways that it could have been avoided, is called "undoing." It's like dropping your ice cream on the ground and then stepping on it for no good reason. It makes you feel worse, it doesn't solve the problem, and now you really can't make anything of it.

In *The Undoing Project* by Michael Lewis, this process is described as being mentally destructive, not only in the moment but for years to come. *"Why did I do that?"* (or any derivative of this phrase) catastrophically keeps you there, punishing you for not having thought things through or done things differently. You can run through endless "undoing" situations, pretending that you can somehow retroactively anticipate the ultimate outcomes and change the ending. This is insane, because what is done is done, but our Dragons like us to ruminate, beating ourselves up for not having seen it coming.

On the *Encyclopedia of Personality and Individual Differences* website, it defines the Undoing Method as *the defense mechanism by which individuals avoid conscious awareness of disturbing impulses by thinking or acting in a way intended to revert ("make un-happen") those impulses, even if only at a symbolic level.*

Ah, there it is again: our defense mechanisms coming to our "rescue." It sounds almost insane to try to revert things back to what they were, and while we can long for this to happen when relationships go sour or we get into a car accident, it is impossible. The past is immovable. It cannot be undone, ever. And yet our brains can become so distressed that it feels like the only way to cope.

Let's say that one day, on your way to work, you are in a rush so you take a short cut. Along the way, you get into a car crash. You can "if only" that one to death: "If only I'd left earlier," or "If only I'd taken the regular route," and so on. I've been in enough car accidents to know precisely how this feels. In one accident, I nearly killed my brother by turning left in front of a speeding car (he was in the passenger seat). If only I'd waited … Luckily, he lived. But I undid that scenario for decades.

After my car crash, I "undid" that singular event over and over, just wishing I'd gone a little bit slower, seen the ice a little bit sooner. In the undoing, I hit "replay" so many times I started to fear driving at all.

Undoing keeps us rooted in the pain of the event but adds guilt on top to make it stick, reminding us over and over again of our shortcomings or poor decision-making. I felt guilt about the damage to the car. I couldn't use that on-ramp for a long time, and you could see my tire tracks down the embankment for years. Rarely do we "undo" good experiences. We like to relive them, but we don't reinterpret the data, crushing our already squished up souls. It's the ones for which you feel personally responsible for the poor outcomes that your Dragon loves to run continuously through your head.

If that isn't horrible enough, building an undoing habit leads to over-apologizing or the avoidance of risk-taking, even just doing things a little bit differently. People who have gotten stuck in this mental mode are the ones who claim to love routine, predictability, and sameness. In reality, they hate all those things, but their fear of doing something out of the ordinary *and* something bad happening is so great that they stick to the ordinary, slogging it out every day. They don't want to feel bad about their decisions, so they make none.

Your Dragon has all of your bad experiences, horrible decisions, destroyed relationships, terrible arguments, and more on tape and is happy to play them over and over again, digging the knife deeper into your heart as it whispers what you *could* have done to prevent the disaster. Oh, the delight it takes in this! And the more you habitually undo events great and small, the stronger your Dragon becomes.

"Yum! Yum!" it says. "Let's play it again, Sam!"

DO WHAT YOU'RE SUPPOSED TO DO

For most of my life, I lived and did what I thought I was "supposed" to. I went to school and tried to fit in, even though the religion I grew up in demanded that I physically look different, with long hair and skirts. No makeup, no jewelry. I couldn't make friends at school because they were all going to hell, but I could try to bring them to the church. That's what good girls do.

I went to university and got good grades. I got married to a God-fearing man. I got a job. I had kids. I wasn't sure what the plan was after that … there seemed like a big gap between kids and retiring, but I figured that was the drill. I started to get in trouble with the church members because I was "supposed" to stay home after I had kids, but we couldn't live on just one income. After Zack, my second, was born, I was told that I had relegated them all to hell because I put them in day care. They'd be led astray for sure, to damnation or worse. I was torn between how good it felt to work and how bad I was to be working. This was just the beginning of the push-pull of doing what I was supposed to versus what I wanted to do. I stuck to the safe route for long enough to get stomach pains and night sweats, terrified that I was letting everyone down and that my children would suffer irreparable damage both in this world and the one beyond.

But I kept trying. My husband and I had people over for dinner. I kept the kids on a schedule. I did my work quietly, never talking about it. I was a good little girl through and through (mostly because I was terrified of what would happen if I wasn't. Again, cancer or a car crash were the favorite choices for what happens if you even THINK about leaving the church, and well, we can see how true that really is).

Along the way, things started to go wrong. I got a job, but it didn't work out, so I quit. Then I got fired from the next one. Then I got fired *again*. Each successive job paid less and less until, one day, I couldn't bear the thought of getting another one; but I was about to get fired for the third time. The only reason I didn't get canned is because the day they were going to kick me out, I quit. Living a "supposed to" life was unraveling, and fast.

My first marriage was not much different, and the outcome no less painful. I thought that I had done the right thing, getting married, but after a few years, it started to fizzle out (we were married wayyyyyy too young and grew apart quickly). By our tenth year, I was miserable in every way. I hated going home. I loved my kids, but I was angry all the time. I'd fly into rages, then wallow in the shame of it.

Soon after I rolled my car, I blew it all up, starting with the church. Those people were wrong: I didn't die. Ha! Take THAT, fearmongers! I left the church, facing an uncertain future, without a support network, friends, or any clue how things would turn out. I might as well have crawled out from a bunker for all I knew how to cope with living a "normal" life. I didn't know how to order cable TV, pay a mortgage, or do much that many people take for granted as easy and routine.

I had no friends. Any relationship I had in the church vanished. I had no friends outside the church. Until the Great Life Blowout, I had deemed everyone evil, sure they would lead me to damnation. I'd considered them dangerous, and now when I needed them, I had no one. I didn't know how to make friends. In nearly every way, I didn't even know where to start.

I left my husband, entering a rebound relationship with someone I thought I could "save" (spoiler: I didn't). That ended badly and stupidly — so stupidly that I refuse to put it in print.

After my final "I quit"/"No, you're fired" fiasco, I started a series of companies, eventually leading to my seven-figure marketing agency. And all along the way, I was absolutely, unequivocally miserable, because I was still stuck trying to figure out if I was living like I was "supposed to." The landscape was different, but I still felt that I had to answer to some "overlord" that set the rules. Instead of the church giving me the rules of how to behave, I looked for industry "experts" and gurus and tried to follow their instructions.

You're supposed to follow a pre-set track, but I couldn't find it. Just fall in line and it will be fine, they said. Even when I was running my marketing agency, supposedly creating my own destiny, I constantly chased the "Two Comma Club" because if you weren't making a million dollars, you were a failure. That's what agencies were supposed to achieve. And so I kept chasing.

But it's the equivalent of living your neighbor's life, your colleague's career, or your competitor's business. It's a life of frustration as you attempt to imitate and monkey the actions and aspirations of others. You're trying to predict your ability to be "successful" based on how others define it, but you never achieve it. And so you chase success, happiness, and love, never feeling in control, always tired. But you keep up pretenses, terrified that someone will discover your fraud.

I learned how to interact with people by reading books. It's one of the reasons I was never diagnosed with autism until my forties. I was a good imitator; yet I found most social interactions confusing and exhausting. Leave me to my books and music and I'm a happy girl! But this was also not acceptable. You're supposed to have a social life, but not too social. Have friends, but not go out too much, and then only with the "approved" friend groups. The rules are legion, changeable, and unpredictable.

"Everyone is doing it" is the social pressure from others to fall in line as well. Not only is our internal monologue restricting our movements and conforming our thoughts to what we believe is the "norm," but socially, we get pressured to be like everyone else too. Fit in, but be yourself. Confusing!

And this is what your Dragon loves the most: confusion. There are rules. They aren't clear, but you still have to follow them. When I hit a million in revenue with my company, I thought I'd feel elated. Instead, I felt defeated. It was a miserable time for me because I had everyone and everything around me that should have made me happy. But the black cloud of confusion, imitation, and exhaustion overtook all other emotions, and I was left empty and flustered.

If the journey to where you want to go is fraught with doubt, pain, confusion, and conforming to standards and routines that aren't natural to you, there is no achievement or accomplishment in the world that will satisfy you.

And your Dragon loves it.

WIRED FOR NEGATIVITY

The main reason your Dragon has a leg up on your GOAT is simple wiring: we're designed to see the negative about 10X more than the positive. When I get my clients to go through how they feel about themselves, a relationship, or their business, they're almost shocked to notice some positive emotions popping up. They thought it was all doom and gloom, and it turns out it's actually got quite a lot of sunshine and unicorns!

This is one of the Dragon's oldest tricks in the evolutionary book. Our negative bent saved us from being crushed, beaten, stabbed, and otherwise killed or poisoned. It's how the strong passed on their genes to the next generation, keeping the species going. But today, there are fewer threats. Life compared to prehistoric times is pretty chill. So why hasn't this part of our brains switched off?

I work with a lot of people who want to break into doing something new and challenging. One of the patterns I've seen is where they are all ready to go with their new "thing," priced, prepared, promoted and ... they stall out. They just don't launch. I've had to have what I call "ass kicking" calls to find out what's behind the hesitation. Ten out of ten times, it's some made-up, fear-based story about why it won't work, no one wants to listen to them, what if it's too expensive, and so on.

Since I don't live in my clients' fear, I see all the upside — the financial freedom, the stress-free living, the confidence and courage taking root and propelling them ever higher.

But all they see is death and destruction, humiliation and rejection, or worse. Their brains detect this new, unfamiliar thing as being the most important thing to avoid, and they will revert to literally anything to avoid it.

I can't blame them, but I won't let them get away with it, either. They're wired to be Eeyore about hard things, using that sad donkey's favorite phrases, like "No one listens to me anyway" or "Most likely to lose anyway." But there's also good news: you can rewire your brain to be less negative. You'll never get rid of it; fear has its moments when it's useful. But when fear holds you back, it's time to tackle the Dragon. I've proven this to be possible countless times; and while it's not easy, it's possible. You just have to want it badly enough because, once again, you'll be not only fighting your Dragon, but the oldest, strongest, and most resilient part of that Dragon.

It's far more effective in marketing to tell people what they'll miss out on if they "don't act now," or how stupid they'll look if everyone is doing it but they're not. Politics takes it a step further with attack ads, knowing people remember negative things said more than anything good anyone's doing in the world. Watch the news much? You might hear about puppy antics on morning shows, but those are forgotten when world hunger, war, and scan-dals erupt on the screen. We're surrounded by horror and sadness, and your Dragon wants you to expose yourself to those messages as much as possible, to absorb them, and learn to be scared.

Think about this: every time you focus on the negative, your Dragon nods its head, thankful you're toeing the line. It gets rattled badly when you see the good that can come out of whatever you're facing and will double down on crushing those thoughts. But the more you think them, the faster you rewire your brain … and the Dragon shrinks just a little bit more.

FAKE COMMITMENT

Your Dragon hates it when you make commitments to do some-thing new and will do anything it can to stop it, by having you use "fake" commitment language. I had a client in today, and all we talked about was shooting a video to post as content on her social media sites. And yet every time we talked about committing to shoot it, she'd freak out, pull back, and say, "Forget it. I don't want to do it."

So, I conducted an experiment. There are two ways we live up to our commitments: how we feel about them, and the actual words we use to describe them. I have an Emotion Wheel I used for my autistic son to help him articulate what he is feeling because while he may have an idea of what's going on in his head, telling me about it is nearly impossible. He doesn't have the words. So, the wheel helps him out.

My client and I went through the words related to "fear," coming up with emotions like inadequate, anxious, overwhelmed, and exposed. Then, again focusing on the resistance to shooting videos, I went through the "happy" emotions list. Turns out that one was *longer* than the "fear"-based emotions list. Until she went through that exercise, though, her ability to see anything positive about recording herself and posting it was nonexistent. We were trying to find a way for her to make a commitment to doing more to promote her business; but until she was able to see *anything* positive about it, there was no action in sight.

Negative emotions are the kryptonite of commitment. If some-thing appears difficult to our brains, the amygdala signals a halt in the proceedings, and we feel strongly compelled to do anything *other* than what we'd committed to do. But missing commitments makes us feel bad, particularly when we commit to do things for others. So, your Dragon has a way around that, clever devil that it is, by creating "fake" commitments.

Let's focus now on the words we use to describe our commitments. Think of something you wanted to commit to, like exercising regularly, eating healthier, doing more productive work, going to bed on time. If you can, go back and think of the language you were using at the time. Were you really committing to it, or were you using non-commitment language that *sounded* like you were going to follow through?

Fake commitment sentences have words that sound good but do not actually give instructions to our brains to take action. We all use them. When I present these in a workshop or on stage, I love to ask people how many of these phrases they'd used that day already. They include, but are not limited to:

- *I want to ...*
- *I hope ...*
- *I wish ...*
- *I'm trying ...*
- *I've got to ...*
- *I have to ...*
- *I need to ...*
- *I should ...*

Absolutely none of those phrases lead to achievements of any kind. Hope is not a strategy. Wishes don't lead to riches. There is doing or not doing; there is no try. You've likely used all of these sentence-starters before, but do you know why they are so dangerous? They make us believe that we are moving toward our goals. We convince ourselves that we're making progress! It's a plan! There are goals! In reality, you're just listening to your Dragon's spin doctors, rationalizing away the reality of your fear so you don't have to see through your commitments. Doing hard work is not fun, it can be scary, and it's often unfamiliar — a recipe for your Dragon to step in and shut down the proceedings. You won't fight the Dragon if you feel like you're feeding your GOAT, and this false pretense repeats in nearly every facet of our lives.

When we use these phrases, we know, in our hearts, there's no way that we're going to follow through. Not a chance. But that makes us feel guilty, and so the spin doctor goes to work, soothing our tiny egos with language that appears to assuage our desires to look like we're doing something. We committed! Isn't that enough?

Later in this book, you'll find how to phrase your thoughts and words in such a way as to guarantee achievements. But until you eradicate these non-commitment, spin doctor-ish thoughts from your vocabulary (spoken and unspoken), your Dragon will win yet more battles, becoming stronger and harder to shrink and control.

"IT'S FINE" (NO, IT'S NOT)

Heather was my first client as a high-performance coach. She is delightful, but when we first started working together, I got more dead-eyes and "go aways" than agreement about where she needed to take her business. Regardless, she always did the work, except when she would say, "It's fine." Heather said, "It's fine" *so often* over the years that I bought her a sweatshirt that said, "*I'm fine. It's fine. Everything is fine.*" When she wore it for the first time, her husband commented on how absolutely perfect it was for her! The words "it's fine" are the equivalent of "shut up, I don't want to talk about this anymore." They kill conversation, preventing anyone from helping you solve a problem or address an issue. I became adept at sidestepping the "it's fine" statements with Heather, challenging her (and so many others like her!) to step past the fear behind the words and address what was really going on. Because it was never fine. Life and business can be hard. "Fine" covers your eyes and ears until the horrible feelings pass.

"It's fine" is the king of avoidance behaviors. It's a deflector, a (false) assurance that all is actually okay, and a passive-aggressive ending to the conversation. Plus, we don't have to do whatever we were told to do because we've "it's fine-d" it away. It accomplishes so much for us that we get very used to using it in all sorts of situations, and yet it is precisely one of the main reasons we stay miserable.

"It's fine" is one of the Great Lies that your Dragon whispers in your ear. If you believe the lie, you don't have to do anything. But in your heart of hearts, you know it's not fine, and those feelings and emotions are left to boil and bubble beneath the surface, surely to show their ugliness at the most inopportune moment in the future. "It's fine" invalidates the way you really feel and crushes your ability to get help. Invalidated feelings turn pain into suffering, and joy into disappointment.

I love animated movies, particularly *The Lego Movie*. In the first one, the adventurers are in Cloud Cuckoo Land, and Princess Unikitty is trying very, very hard to hold herself together as the Bad Cop is destroying it. She repeats over and over "Stay positive! Stay positive!" When her world is finally destroyed, and she's watching the remnants float past, she tries that again, adding in some other mantras and memories that make her happy — cotton candy, bubble gum, and so on in a vain attempt to make herself feel better.

But it's never enough, and it doesn't work. She's crushed but keeps all those feeling jammed deep inside. At the end of the movie, Emmet is getting the snot kicked out of him, and she once again does the "stay positive" bit until she can't anymore, hits the kitty-rage button, destroys the place, and saves Emmet. I think she felt better after that.

I like the way Bill O'Hanlon describes "thinking positive" in *Do One Thing Different*: it's like spraying poop with glitter. Sure, it looks nice, but it still smells, and the longer you hold onto it, the longer the stink sticks to you. "It's fine" is a version of thinking positive and doesn't actually resolve the underlying issue. So, the stink remains, piled ever higher.

We cannot pretend we don't have any problems. We often try to mask our pain so that others won't see it, but the list of suicides, drug and alcohol abuses, and other tragedies speaks loudly of this failure. Social media factors largely in this charade, with filters, Photoshop, and other manipulations of the truth allowing the false story to pervasively shadow our news feeds. "It's fine," our news feed says as we sit, confused and alone, at the keyboard.

In the years since I wrapped up my social media agency, I have posted less and less online, preferring to live and enjoy every moment instead of worrying about chronicling it. This has helped to curb my own habit of making it look all rosy when inside I wanted to give up. My Dragon kept that online game of pretend going for a very long time, and with every word I wrote and picture I posted, I *knew* it wasn't the whole truth. But my spin doctor was a wily little devil and convinced me that "everyone else" was doing it, so I had permission to proceed.

Your Dragon sings a happy song when it hears you utter, "I'm fine," continuing your charade and holding up your façade. It knows that as long as you keep that rhetoric going, nothing will change, and all will be "safe" in your internal world. Your Dragon will help you hold up your mask, giving strength and power to this destructive habit.

DEFLECTION (NOT TAKING COMPLIMENTS)

Another form of deflection is refusing to accept compliments or gifts, batting them aside with disgust or embarrassment. Ashley, a dear client, friend, and confidante, spent years accumulating unopened thank-you gifts in her basement, feeling like she didn't deserve them. A successful, incredible real estate maven, her reputation as a powerhouse preceded her everywhere, and yet the compliments or gifts that confirmed this made her squirm. She felt she was just doing her job (which she was, magnificently). So why would anyone see the need to give her something for it? They'd already paid her from the commission … and anything more was embarrassing to her.

Gay Hendricks explains in his book *The Big Leap* that this deflection comes from a disconnect between how we value ourselves and what others see in us. When someone does a great job for us, we often want to show appreciation. Gifts, compliments, or giving our time are just a few of the ways to do that. The problem arises when the gift exceeds the value we ascribe to ourselves; and instead of creating feelings of love and warmth, it generates a sense of embarrassment and even shame, and those are feelings we want to get rid of as fast as possible. We question whether we actually did the job the givers say we did. And so, we reject the gifts, saying, "Oh, stop it," or outright deny the compliments. We send everyone home if they've shown up to offer their time or assistance. "I can totally do this myself," I hear Ashley say.

The wider the value gap between how we see ourselves and how others see the value of what we provide, the more vehemently we refuse what is being offered. When Ashley told me of her basement full of unopened gifts, the work assigned for that week was to open them all. Hundreds of dollars in gift cards, beautiful gifts — some of them painstakingly handmade — were revealed. She had to then deal with the guilt of not having thanked people at the time, and to her credit, she sat down and wrote everyone a

thank-you note, asking for forgiveness for her delay in responding. That's powerhouse action right there — overcoming the feeling of having waited too long to say thanks but doing it anyway. Most Dragons would never let that happen!

I often teach this concept with leadership groups. To showcase how to overcome these Dragon moments, I make people pair off and give each other a heartfelt compliment. It's both hilarious and sad to watch. One person says something nice, and the other person cringes, closes their eyes, sticks out their tongue, or looks away. Then they shout, "No! Do it again! Do it again! I'll get it this time!" They keep at it until they can handle the compliment with a straight face and utter a heartfelt thanks.

It's weird to say that it takes practice to take a compliment or gift, but it's true. If your self-worth doesn't match up with how highly other people see you,

you're doomed to discomfort every time something positive happens to you. The positive reference doesn't align with the poor identity you'd given yourself. Your Dragon loves that cringing and often twists the knife a little more by throwing in a few thoughts about how you really don't deserve anything, let alone the kind words or gifts being offered.

Your Dragon will try to keep the disparity as wide as possible because if you remedied it, you'd have more confidence to do things that are different and therefore unsafe. When a compliment comes your way, it will whisper to you that you don't deserve it. You're not worthy. You're nothing. Hand it back. Deflect. Do not accept it. And the pain lingers because you want to acknowledge what is being given, but you can't. And the Dragon wins another battle.

NAME THE DRAGON

Ask yourself a question: Can you give words to how you feel about yourself right now? Take a moment and write them down. Most people stop at "happy, sad, mad" so try to be a little more specific.

I often find it far simpler to experience life, not feel it. This behavior is rooted in my past, and my autism. The feelings I have rolling around in my head are complex and hard to identify. I find it hard to express how I feel, despite being a pro at getting every-one *else* to dig into their emotions through my coaching practice. It's always easier to get everyone else to do the hard work, isn't it? As I was going through the autism diagnosis process, my psychologist, the wonderful Dr. Hendry, asked me how I felt about a particularly distressing situation I was experiencing. We'd just finished hashing it out, yet my mind drew a complete blank on how precisely I'd say I felt about it. I couldn't believe I had no words. I *always* have words. But the only thing that came to mind was "Sad" with a question mark at the end.

Without the actual words that described how I felt, I was completely unable to process and move on from that difficult situation. My brain held onto the pain, without having the ability to move through the feelings. And yet naming these emotions is the gateway to inner calm and being better able to handle any situation, no matter how difficult. It's a game I now call "Name the Dragon."

There's a process I have taught for years, which defines how we need to start several steps before "working harder" to get the life we want. My process used to be four steps, but I've recently added another step at the very beginning. Let me explain how to read the chart you'll see below. We'll go from right to left, then back again.

At the far right is our reality. Life as it is today. Most often, if we don't like where we are, we figure we're just not working hard enough, so we dial that up — and quickly burn out. Turns out, you have to back that "Life Train" up several stations before you can truly start changing your reality, and it has nothing to do with working harder. Most often, you work *less*.

Here's how it works.

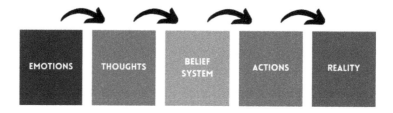

First Station: Emotions
Emotions: These are the main drivers of what we actually think. If our emotions and feelings are all over the place, or if we cannot describe or identify them, the entire process that follows is a mess. This is why we feel unsure of ourselves: we haven't got the root of our life under control. When you name your emotions, you begin to claim them, and take their power away.

Second Station: Thoughts
Thoughts are generated by our emotions. This is where we fall into the habit of making up stories about ourselves, others, the world, our work, our future, and get ourselves in a right mess.

Third Station: Beliefs
Thoughts thought often enough become our belief system. As you can see by this point, if your thoughts are messing you up, your hopes of living a life you deserve are shot to bits. You believe what you tell yourself. Full stop.

Fourth Station: Actions

That belief system then feeds your actions. If you go into a prospecting call having told yourself that no one wants to listen to you and you're going to screw it up anyway, you'll start the call with, "Sorry to bother you …" as opposed to, "Got a minute? I have something really cool to tell you!"

Fifth and Final Station: Reality

How you act creates your world. Manifestation, faith, and hope are all lovely, but if you look up the gurus of those theories and methodologies, they are *imploring* you to take action. But you literally can't, won't, or will avoid doing so if your emotions are in tatters, your thoughts are self-defeating, and your belief system is toxic. The technical term for having a bag of electric eels for emotions is "emotional dysregulation." The definition is simple: *an emotional reaction that is overly intense in comparison with the situation that triggered it.* If you don't know how you feel, your brain will just go with what it knows best and either freak out, shut down, or run away. Big emotions are the toughest to name and process. We often want to push them aside. We might get in trouble if we're angry, and fear is debilitating. But when your emotions get stuffed down, they turn on you. With nowhere to go, your feelings start to manifest as self-hatred.

Brené Brown thinks that most people live life *"waiting for the other shoe to drop."* Big life decisions can make us feel vulnerable, afraid, anxious, and a whole host of other things, big and small. And it's not only bad situations that cause these reactions, either. Her list included:

- Having a baby
- Getting a promotion
- Getting engaged
- Thinking about a romantic relationship
- Standing over children while they sleep

These experiences can generate powerful and often conflicting emotions. She describes "foreboding joy" as the feeling that while something good just happened, something horrible would follow. Your Dragon loves to make you feel that all the good in your world will end. "Everything can be taken away," it chants.

I've had clients double their income in one year, only to worry incessantly about whether this was just a blip or a lucky break. Those who believed this horrible story saw their incomes drop precipitously the following year. It was hard to watch, and nothing I said or did could stop the fall. Their Dragon had taken over.

When we are faced with the truly unfamiliar and our emotions go haywire, we hit overwhelm. As the wave of emotions wash over you, they become physical manifestations — fast heart rate, sweaty palms, clenched teeth and fists, or tears. The first step in getting through these tough times is to give words to what you feel. Then, it's time to deal with the physical symptoms.

I've had numerous situations in which I have become so angry and so upset that I've tearfully come to Marc saying, *"I don't know what to do with this anger."* It had nowhere to go. I tried to get rid of it or suppress it, attempting to stop feeling anything. But that wasn't the way it worked. Until relatively recently, I didn't know that it was *integrating* those feelings *within me* that helped them flow away: that and punching a pillow or beating up my punching bag with a baseball bat. Dr. Hendry, my amazing psychologist, explained that this physical exertion helps release the pent-up energy of these gigantic emotions. It is only after these big emotions subside that I can find logic again and think more clearly. But I have to go through the entire process to get there — become aware of the emotions, name them, and if I have excess energy, to exert myself until it's gone. My Dragon has been my master for most of my life, keeping me amped up, instead of calming down.

The Dragon is a genius at creating emotional disasters and derailed Life Trains. I imagine it as the conductor of a huge orchestra, with each "musician" in charge of a particular emotion or feeling. Depending upon the situation at hand, it will create a symphony of dissonance and pain, triggering past events to come rocketing into the present, reminding us of the pain and fear from our past.

A FINAL WORD ABOUT YOUR DRAGON

In *Harry Potter and the Prisoner of Azkaban*, the kids are asked to face their greatest fear and laugh at it. One by one, they're marched up to a shaking, thumping cabinet, inside of which is a Boggart: the thing they fear the most. Not only that, everyone in the class must conjure their fear in front of their peers, adding the twin terrors of judgment and mockery into the mix.

Once their fear erupts from the cabinet, they have to quickly turn it into something to laugh at to make it small, funny, ridiculous. The spell is "riddiku-lus!," and if they shout it just right, their fear changes. And what really finishes it off is laughter. One by one, their fears turn from terrifying to the amusing: Professor Snape suddenly wears women's clothes and carries a handbag, giant spiders sprout roller skates, snakes turn into clowns.

Shrinking your Dragon is the same process: making unnecessary fears so ridiculous as to be not worth a minute of your time. To make big, scary emotions like fear, anger, and guilt your allies. Your time should be spent living your GOAT life.

How long has your Dragon been eating at your table, feeding you lies, stories, and terrors? And for how much longer should it have pride of place at your side?

The choice is yours. Later in this book, there will be strategy after strategy you can use to move it further and further away from you, opening up more space for your GOAT. So, let's see what that can look like, shall we?

BOOK 1, PART 2

ARE YOU LIVING YOUR GOAT LIFE?

HOW TO KNOW
IF YOU'RE LIVING YOUR GOAT LIFE

T he first time I truly realized the full extent of my potential GOAT-ness, it felt like thunder. I'd been working steadily at shrinking my Dragon, but still felt like I was being held back. I was running my high-performance coaching business, which was light years better than my agency. I'd simplified my business model and had a minimal support team. I thought I really had my life together … and yet something was wrong. Again. I was really getting sick of this feeling. But what was it? I got out my psychological hunting gear and started searching for what was "off" in my life.

My son is autistic, and high school has been an interesting ride. As I began to hunt for reasons for my malaise, I looked to areas of stress. At the time, he was one of them. I was at the end of my rope. How could I get him to believe that getting more than a 56% was both necessary and motivating for his future? I suggested to his therapist that we do a session just her and me, and she readily agreed. At the end of our appointment, she referred me to a video about autism, kids, high school, and how I could parent my child more effectively and with less frustration. Maybe this was the source of my happiness block! I had high hopes.

The Wednesday night after that session, I was sitting in my office getting ready to teach my group program at 7:00 pm. I had some time, so I decided to watch the video. It was only about thirty minutes long, and I had just enough time. I desperately wanted to understand my son and how to help him get the most out of life, and this video sounded promising. I didn't want to be stressed by his situation, and figured this was what was causing my feelings of being off-kilter. I pressed play and sat back in my chair.

The highly engaging British psychologist, Professor Tony Attwood, entertained me for the first half of the video, helping me make more sense of autism in boys, particularly at my son's age. He talked about how they see the world, and how I can adjust parenting him. There were ideas on how to relate to him, motivate him, and relax. Great!

Then at precisely twenty minutes and six seconds in, my entire world went on tilt.

Professor Attwood began talking about the "invisible end of the spectrum": girls. And for the next ten minutes, he perfectly and accurately described *me*. I sat there, tea halfway to my face, my mind blown into a million pieces. Wait a sec: *I'm autistic????* I always figured Zack got it from my ex's side. His brother was *definitely* on the spectrum. But ME????

Turns out, girls present autism very differently than boys. We're often not diagnosed until later in life, typically in our forties. From here on in, I shall refer to this group as "we," myself now being an active and thriving member of the group I'd unknowingly been a part of all my life. It's also important to note that once you've met one autistic person, you've met exactly *one* — each of us is different in the way we are wired, but there are commonalities that link us as a group.

Among other things, women with autism prefer to wear black (colors are confusing), and ADHD is often a huge factor. We struggle with friendships, partnerships, and explaining exactly how we're feeling. If we've inadvertently offended someone just by being ourselves, we are emotionally devastated. We just don't always see things coming. We imitate things — fashions, hairstyles, makeup, and so on — because we don't have the capacity to know what looks "good." I learned how to socialize with people by reading a massive number of books and pretending I was certain characters to try to elicit the same responses I saw on the page. In junior high school, I read *Sweet Valley High* because I thought I could figure out how to act and be accepted. I didn't have the "perfect tan" but I was about 5'6", so I had that in common with the twins in the books. Close enough.

This entire experience of coming to see myself as autistic was what I had been looking for. I was "off " because I wasn't fully aware of who I really *was*. My feelings of being "off " had nothing to do with anything, other than how I viewed and accepted myself. Watching this video and recognizing my autism felt like the final epiphany in my string of epiphanies since leaving the cult and blowing up my life. It has given me something that nothing and no one has ever been able to deliver: self-forgiveness and a power to live on my own terms like never before. I felt whole for the first time.

It explains why I kept getting fired and never understood or played office politics the right way. I'd piss people off, get written up, and get in trouble. It was constant, and I had no idea why I kept tripping up in that way. It explains why I never want to hang out with people I consider friends. I *never* call them because I don't know how to end a call without thinking I've offended the person. The ones I've told about my autism feel closer to me than ever. They accept this about me, and we have hilarious codes I can use when I need to end a conversation without thinking I've caused offense.

I have never felt confident with style and still can't figure out what to do with my hair. And it explains why no one ever knew I was autistic: with all my reading and imitating, coupled with being a master apologizer, I flew under the radar. Until this thunderous moment, I never understood how to use this autistic superpower to live a life of happiness, fulfillment, and joy. I accepted my wiring. I accepted my personality. I accepted all of me.

But now I had this power, and whoooooo boy — here we GOAT!

As I pieced together more about how my brain was wired and what I loved and hated, I realized certain things had to go: I was still imitating and attempting to be like "everyone else." I dissolved my last outstanding partnership. I explained that I wasn't built for working with people. It was a classic *"it's not you, it's me"* kind of moment, but I truly meant it. I'd made the last few months of the partnership miserable for myself and for her; it had to end for both of our sakes. This ending didn't feel like failure anymore. It felt like a gift.

With the final fetters of my imitated life unshackled for the last time, I stepped into my, true GOAT-ness. I created programs that would work *with* my brain, not against it. I forgave my past self, refusing to allow the pain to resurface as it had for decades. I finally believed I was not broken. There was nothing wrong with me after all. I became 100% okay with being an "army of one" in my business, instead of bowing to the pressure of building a team to be "successful" in the eyes of my industry gurus. I blessed my days with work that appealed to my inner GOAT so that it danced, sang, and bleated its little head off.

This is what it means to live on your own terms, as your true GOAT. As I fully accepted who I was, how I was wired, what it meant, and how to build my future so that I lived solely in a way that worked for me — regardless of what everyone else said or did — my Dragon became so small that it could fit in the palm of my hand. The tiny puffs of smoke hardly made an impression on me anymore. No heat. It had no power.

I know my Dragon will never be gone. It still serves a purpose. I really don't want to get eaten by a modern-day equivalent of a saber-toothed tiger, and I like being able to breathe and hear my heartbeat. Fear, anger, and guilt are still helpful tools, but they don't stop me from being happy, wealthy, and fulfilled anymore. Now it's your turn. How do you know that you're living *your* full GOAT life? The next part of this book will outline how you can tell if you're on the path of your greatness, or not. Don't despair if nothing seems to line up with how you're living right now. Keep going because in Book 3, I will show you how to make it all happen in your unique, GOAT-y way!

WHAT LIVING A GOAT LIFE MEANS

I often get asked, "How do I know if I'm truly living my 'GOAT' life?" There are lots of ways, such as (but not limited to) the following:

> To live a GOAT life is to *act* before you *feel.*
> It is to *decide* instead of taking instructions.
> It is to *create* instead of blindly following orders.
> It is to *believe* before there is *proof.*
> It is to *create* an identity before your *belief systems* are even in place.
> It is to know that something might not work but to *try it anyway.*
> It is to *choose,* not wait to be *chosen.*
> It is to *act* before there is *confidence* in the action.

It is to realize that *motivation* is an after-effect of *moving* toward a goal.

It is to *listen* to advice, but discard it if it doesn't *fit*.

It is to be radically *open-minded* to only make what you're doing *better*.

It is to accept, reject, or limit *exposure* to people based on their *contribution* to your life.

It is to know that hard work turns into *passion*, not the other way around.

It is to set *boundaries* and protect them at all costs.

It is to know when "yes" and "no" are appropriate and *not bend your rules* just because someone might not like the limits that have been set.

There are many more, some you may already live by. Building a GOAT life based on these tenets is well within your reach. The trick is to stop waiting for someone to give it to you. Storm the castle and take control from the Dragon.

FEELING LIMITLESS

Steven factors large in this book because we've worked on so many things in so many ways. So, here's another Steven story. It's one of my favorites.

I'd been helping Steven create an organizational structure that gives him more time to focus on his passions beyond his brokerage. He just didn't know what "his passions" were. More accurately, he knew but was afraid to go anywhere near them, full of fears that no one wanted to listen to him or find what he had to share useful, let alone something they'd pay for.

One of Steven's many talents lies in creating the precise success models for real estate brokerages, saving them hundreds of thousands of dollars, increasing profits, and opening up more time for the owners and managers to scale their business. He'd developed a consulting package that would basically install the entire backend system for a brokerage, and he'd then train the owners and managers on how to run it. It was priceless.

Right before he was to launch, his Dragon went wild. First, he priced it at one-third of what it was worth. It took a LOT of convincing to get him to believe that people would pay five figures for a system that would save them hundreds of thousands of dollars and a massive amount of wasted time.

Then the challenge was his mental nemesis: no one wants to listen to him and no one would buy it. This turned into a two-month stall out where he futzed around with one client but didn't prospect for more. He didn't think he had the credibility or the time. He needed a website. He needed a bigger social media presence. He just kept shoving the launch date away until one day, he didn't have any more crap to shovel. He had a list of people to call. I was going to fly to Kansas myself and beat him with his stapler if he didn't make those calls. He agreed to two by the next week. Fine. Two it is.

He got seven. In the three weeks after, he added five more. Remember, this is the Steven whose eyes disappear when he smiles. I can happily say that I haven't seen his baby blues in a while.

When he described what his new business venture meant to him, he said, "I finally feel like there are no limits to what I can do, how much I can make, and what my future holds."

BAM! GOAT-struck! He found it! Eureka!

This is how you become your GOAT. Not any GOAT — *your* GOAT.

It's not pretty. It's not a straight line. Your Dragon freaks out in a BIG way, but if you keep going, your GOAT emerges stronger, louder, and with a limitlessness you cannot describe unless you've felt it, like Steven did.

THERE'S A GOAT IN EACH OF US

There is a GOAT within you, and it really wants you to pay attention to it. You can't Google "how to become a GOAT." You can research how people like Serena Williams, Tom Brady, Michael Jordan, and Tiger Woods became GOATs in their own way, but your way will be different. You can take pieces from their stories and weave them into your own, but only if they fit. This is not the imitation game. GOATs throw away anything that doesn't jibe with their wiring, desires, passions, and talents, not because those things are bad, but they're not for them. This is a common refrain: "It's just not for me."

Think back to when you were a child and you created some-thing: a piece of art, maybe a decorated toilet paper roll or batteries wrapped in masking tape with faces on them (my brother's favorite). How proud were you of that art — that thing *you* did with *your* hands? Or the story you thought up and wrote with all your favorite characters?

There is joy in the creation of the road to your own GOAT, but only you can find it, only you can build it, and only you know what's at the end.

This book is not intended to simply inspire and motivate, though that should happen naturally. It is different because inspiration and motivation appear *after* you start doing something — not before. So, I literally can't motivate you. But you can. Your GOAT can. You just have to get started.

As you read through the next few chapters, I encourage you to take notes, jotting down the areas in which you want to scale up your GOAT-ness. Then, when you hit Book 3 with all the strategies and suggestions on how to live your best life in the happiest and most profitable way possible, you'll already know where to start. So, get your pen and paper ready. I like to call your notebook your "GOAT-book." You're about to make a plan to increase your greatness to become the unique and amazing human who's been dying to get out of your cage and step into the light.

TALENTS AND SKILLS

I was hosting a workshop recently in Wisconsin. The work the people were supposed to be doing was about what talents they possessed and what skills were required so they could spend more time on the things at which they naturally excelled.

This is not an easy exercise. We don't often think we have any talent at all, and yet we do. Mine is being able to detect patterns from what people are telling me, go in my brain's Rolodex of suggestions and ideas, and come up with questions or strategies to unblock my client from their current stuck-ness. That's my *talent*. I then hone the *skills* necessary to showcase my talent. I study how to be a better coach, I read voraciously, I hire my own coaches and psychologists and learn from them. I find better questions to ask, getting deeper into someone's resistance to bring out their inner greatness. I learn to be a better listener. I tend to talk too much.

One gentleman at the workshop stated that he was really good at recruiting, just not at the prospecting calls. Once someone was in front of him, his conversion rate was nearly 100%. So, his talent was in making the prospect feel like this is where they belonged … but then he got stumped. He hated making calls. He couldn't really use his talent because his skill set was missing some mojo. His frustration was palpable, and his tablemates had nothing for him.

I asked a simple question: What if you didn't have to make calls? What if you used a different set of skills? What if you invited prospects to events, workshops, teaching opportunities, career nights, and so on, and for those interested in learning more, just get them to schedule a call? There are any number of ways *other* than calling that you can use to recruit. He was so fixated on the one skill he thought he needed that he forgot about other ways that were way more in tune with his brain, his wiring, and his passions. He'd be far more successful for the simple reason that he actually liked to go about things in a way he enjoyed.

At another table, a woman's talent was taking absolute chaos in someone's office or business and reorganizing it into processes, systems, and projects that flowed easily and clearly. Her skills were based on expanding or perfecting strategies and methodologies she could use to help as many people as possible. Not everyone wants their business organized in the same way, and she had to accommodate that. Her talent was calming the chaos. The skills she needed to step into and perfect were studying and applying various systems, technologies, and researching human behavior so she could convince people to adopt the changes she suggested.

Talent + Skills = GOAT living!

When you identify what comes naturally and easily to you and get over the fact that "easy" is not "bad," the world becomes a much safer and way more entertaining place. A lot of people stray from their greatness because it just seems so simple. Surely, everyone else finds it just as easy. This is yet another falsehood your Dragon wants you to believe, but a GOAT knows to challenge that precept and stick to the easy, happy work. Life isn't a grind and hustle. It's supposed to be a joy.

Lee, one of my clients, has a talent with talking to people and engaging in conversations that lead to deals. He prospects by taking people out for lunch. He's not retired yet, but he wants to feel like he is. Social outings do the trick! That's his business plan. Then he follows up, does the deals, keeps going with the lunches, and makes good money.

Liam has a talent for helping people overcome their limiting beliefs. Having come through a tremendous amount of trauma and tough experiences, he knows a few things about fear. He hones his coaching skills by learning great questions and how to help people move past what is blocking them.

GOATs cultivate their talents and skills, adding and deleting as necessary — especially deleting. We can be like skill hoarders, building up a library of knowledge that becomes useless within hours. Or we have rows and rows of "shelf-help" books, that we bought with the best of intentions, but without the drive for greatness, they remain on the shelf, untouched.

LIVING LIFE ON YOUR TERMS

The phrase "live only on your terms" sounds fantastic. Wonderful. Dreamy. But how do you even come up with these terms, and what does it mean to live by them when you do?

We spend far too much time and energy trying to figure out the world's rules of engagement with friends, family, loved ones, work, school, and more. And just when you think you've figured out the pattern, the goalposts move, and you're left stranded again, trying to make sense of your world.

A true GOAT claims no territorial boundaries other than the ones they create themselves. They write their own rule books, declaring these rules as law, day in, day out, living and breath-ing them every second. There is one author: *them*. There is one standard to which they seek to achieve greatness, happiness, and fulfillment: *theirs*. They are in complete control of their day, spending their time wisely and carefully choosing the people they let into their circles. The rules never change, unless they want them to. There is no confusion.

For the people they let into their world, there are boundaries — things they will accept and things they will not tolerate. They get to decide what the consequences are and how they are meted out. They communicate clearly and articulately to everyone so there is no misunderstanding: their rules, their lives.

They are not dictators, but rather clear on the things they want to see in their day, refusing drama and chaos and embracing the joy and peace that comes with knowing that the world can go to the dogs, but they'll be able to handle it.

Who is drawing the map of your life? Is it you or a committee that push and pull and shove you all over the place, forcing you into the boxes that make *them* feel comfortable? If you attempt to live according to the desires or pressures of someone else, they get to redraw your map, whenever and however they want. The goalposts move, and your stability is shot, making you a prime candidate for an ambush.

Those who live life on their terms hold the pen and never let it go. My Dad recently said that it's not so much about saying "no" all the time, but rather disclosing the things to which he and Mom would say "yes" and sticking to it. It is easy to be peaceful when you are in control of the rules of your life — how you live, who you bring in or haul out, how you go about your day, what you *do* in that day, and so on.

Think of the GOATs you know. They do this all the time, unapologetically.

Michael Jordan wrote his own map through an incredible dedication to practice, mental toughness, and a desire to win — even and especially after being cut from his high school basketball team. As one of the greatest basketball players of all time, he was determined to push not only himself but also his entire team into greatness. He even *left* basketball to try baseball, which didn't work, but whatever — he did it because he wanted to. He'd still be playing if the debacle at the end of his career with the Bulls hadn't pulled the rug out from under him and his incredible team. He then went and did more — on his terms because he liked to. Serena Williams and her sister Venus defied the rules of how women were "supposed" to play, bringing a level of excitement to tennis that has brought the popularity of women's tennis to the same level (and some would say beyond) as men's. She had a kid and kept winning. She has a supportive husband who wasn't jealous of her fame. She continues to expand her empire as she sees fit. Recently retired, we know that tennis will never be the same ever again, because of her.

Tom Brady still plays (as of the moment I'm writing this unless he has since retired, unretired, retired again, etc.) at the age of forty-five after having been selected 199th in his draft year. His focus is not on the typical training schedule that QBs traditionally follow; instead, he is focusing primarily on nutrition, recovery, and flexibility. Quarterbacks aren't "supposed" to play at his age. The rule books are clear. But he doesn't care because he holds his own pen.

The question to ask yourself today is how many pens are out there, scribbling away on your life map? Do you even *have* a pen? Your Dragon hates it when you take all the pens back, but that's precisely what you have to do: set your rules of "no" and "yes" (with a few "heck yeahs!" sprinkled in). This will make your GOAT strong with firm footings and solid boundaries.

FEELINGS AND FREAK-OUTS

We often encourage our kids to manage their feelings. They're expressive little things, and we want them to do it well. Trouble is, we forget to take our own advice. As adults, we don't spend a lot of time discussing our feelings. Support and conversations around mental health have grown in recent years, but you don't have to have a mental health issue to be an emotional wreck.

People living their GOAT lives have a firm grip on precisely how they feel, not because they are particularly emotional people: they know how to clearly identify and process their emotions. There will be no amygdala hijack situations. They will retain 100% functionality at all times, regardless of stress, aggression, fear, anxiety, or anger. They feel these things but process them before a hijack situation gets underway.

Not only do emotionally regulated people identify and clarify what they feel, but they learn from it. In Brené's *Atlas of the Heart*, she talks about needing to pull up a chair and sit with our feelings to understand why they're showing up and then ask ourselves what there is to learn. My psychologist repeatedly reminds me that I don't have to "get rid of" my emotions; I need to process and integrate them within me so my body and mind learn how to deal with them. My inclination is to push my feelings away. I don't want them. But that just keeps them inside, building to boiling points that spill over in the most ungraceful ways.

Therapy has helped me to find coping mechanisms and strategies to identify and deal with how I feel. I didn't know I needed this until I started delving into the Life Train process and saw how integral our emotions are in creating stability in our daily lives. We cannot see what we cannot see, and it often takes a trained specialist to guide us into a higher level of understanding. Avoiding things, worrying, and generating massive anxiety are not the path to a full life. Labelling our feelings is important in starting the process. In the next section of this book, you'll find several strategies to guide you to a greater feeling of being in control of your day-to-day emotions and how to avoid derailment when the big ones hit.

Clarity is the first of the 6 High Performance Habits outlined in Brendon Burchard's *High Performance Habits* that generate a happy and fulfilled life. And clarity is not just about setting goals: it's about how you behave, how you think about yourself, and how you feel about where you are and where you're going. Pure clarity is a deep understanding of the emotions that swirl within, naming them so they can't sneak up on you, and challenging the thoughts that come up. Without this, the world appears to be cloudy and your next step unsure.

GOATs also know how to take any emotion that is "if only …" or "what if …"-based and bring it into the present moment where they can actually deal with it. We can spend our days in the past, regretting and fretting about what we've done or said. Or we can hang out in a fictitious and frightening future of "what if 's" that can scare us into paralysis. Or we can choose the GOAT path and stick to what's right in front of us!

GOATs know how to use deep breathing to bring them back into the moment because their breath can only be in one place: where they are, right now. When you combine emotional regulation with deep breathing or meditation, you can never experience an amygdala hijack, since your emotions just never get that out of whack. I'll show you more on this soon.

IMPACT OVER INCOME

When I began running my marketing agency back in 2012, I focused on one thing: making money. Granted, I was deeply in debt, so this wasn't about greed; it was about survival. But as the years went on and I made more and more, growing my team to fourteen wonderful souls all across the world, the emotions behind that drive became increasingly dark. I worried constantly about keeping up with competitors in my field, researching, and studying the social networking world with all its changes, pivots, and algorithmic updates.

I worried day and night (particularly at night) about where my next client would come from and whether I would make enough to pay myself, let alone my team, next month. Did I have a good enough brand? Did people know and like me enough?

These mostly midnight mental meanderings were exhausting, and after eight years of running the agency, I realized I had to do something drastic. I had worked too hard, too long, and in abject misery nearly the entire time. And even after I reached my money goal, I felt empty and *still miserable.*

As I sat one evening on our couch with Marc, I took note of all the things I had: a house, a car, a motorcycle, great kids, a thriving business … and I still felt empty, even though I had so much to be grateful for.

The question was, *why* didn't it matter? Was being "good" at something not enough?

Then the answer hit me: No, it wasn't enough to just be "good" at something. But that now opened a giant can of worms: what *was* going to be enough and what was I after in the first place? What was really important to me?

As I tossed this in my head, I realized that the work I wanted had to be more than just good marketing campaigns, which I saw as a tiny corner of a business's foundation. Important, but not everything. I wanted people to feel they were competent, successful, happy, and wealthy. I wanted to do work that mattered to me so I could show others how to do work that mattered to *them.* I wanted both sides of the coin to be valuable.

I hunted and researched and eventually landed on high performance coaching. Broad enough to encompass an entire business, based on science, focusing on getting people to do the work, not just attend sessions, to make themselves feel better. It was a bumpy start, as my reputation was founded on social media marketing, and getting people to make the switch took time.

But the biggest switch was what *drove* me in my new business. As I pivoted more and more into high performance coaching, I was determined not to fall into the misery trap. There was only one way to do that: *impact over income thinking.* My agency was "income" driven — afraid of where my money was going to come from, where my clients were, and keeping up with the financial Joneses. Living based on "impact" is to build a business that delivers such incredible results for your clients that you attract as many as you want. You even end up making more money, simply because what you do is good for those you serve.

That sounds beautiful, but my execution was ugly. I was terrified. I would sit at my desk, gripping the edge, repeating "Impact over income, it's going to be okay" over and over again. I had to believe this would turn out better than my agency. I had to believe in my ability to create such insanely good results for my clients that they'd stay with me, refer me, and so on. Could I do it? I wouldn't know until I tried.

Within the first six months, I'd gotten to six figures, and while I wasn't making a million like my agency, I was taking home ten times what I used to. I didn't have a team to pay, and my processes were simple. By year two, I was paying down debt like a demon, finally contributing to my retirement fund so that I might not have to work till I'm 100.

Robert Sharma describes this process perfectly:

> *"Lasting happiness comes from the size of our impact, not the extent of our income. Real fulfillment is a product of the value we create and the contribution we make, not of the car we drive or the house we buy. And I've learned that self-worth is more important that net worth."*

It's all I think about now: self-worth over net worth. How can I keep making what I have even better? What impact do I want to have for my clients? I trust implicitly that the money will come not because I have proof, but because this is the way to being most at peace and in control. I can't predict what others will do, but I can predict how hard I work and what I create and how valuable it is to others. GOATs know how to measure value, because they use their own yardsticks.

INVITE – DON'T CHASE – SUCCESS (IMPACT OVER INCOME CONT'D)

Success and happiness flee at the same velocity at which you chase them. Most often, you're chasing what you *think* is success, but really, it's just an empty dream. Even if you catch it, you feel nothing; the journey wasn't worth it. You feel even worse for having achieved it. I've been there countless times, and so as I ventured further into an impact-driven business, I decided to change things up a bit more. The trick is to invite success and joy to dinner, not chase after them like some lovelorn teenager. Part of this is the impact over income perspective: focus on your incredible work instead of fleeing from the fear of running out of money or not keeping up with the guy on your Instagram feed.

Living an impact-driven life is tough to start, but once you get the hang of it, things go pretty smoothly. To up the challenge, GOATs take it to the next level.

They add in faith that even though they don't know how things will work out, they know that if they tell their brain to focus on what they want, repeatedly, then the opportunity will arise. They just have to be ready and watching. By entering the thing they want into their mental Search Bar, their brain's reticular activation system will ping when a result comes up!

I tried to write my first book, *Think Again*, six times before I finally succeeded. I'd peter out around 5,000 words, unsure of how to go on. So, I took a sticky note, wrote "book" on it, and stuck it on my wall right above my computer screen. I'd stare at it daily. I wasn't sure *how* it was going to happen, but I knew somehow if I kept asking my brain to look for opportunities, one would arrive. I stopped chasing it. I waited for it.

It came in the form of a Facebook ad from a publishing company, and lo and behold, I have an international bestseller! I could have pushed on by myself and struggled, but I lacked the skills to actually make that happen. When I started to relax and let my brain do the work and believe in the process, it happened. I've tried it since with other things — people I wanted to meet, income goals I wanted to hit just so I could say I could. You name it, I've used this process of inviting success instead of fretting and sweating about it.

GOATs know this secret. It's one of the reasons they're so chill. Why stress about things when you know they'll come to you? You can't rush every agenda because you're not in control of every aspect of the world. If you relax your death grip on the controls of life and stop trying to force things, you begin to use your brain's power by telling it what you want it to focus on. You'll find that the things you've always wanted have been in front of you all along. You just didn't see them in your blind panic about life.

GROWTH MINDSETS

Remember fixed mindsets? The ones where people say, "I'm this way. I always have been, and I always will be, so there. Ha!" It's hard to argue with people who think this way and often not worth the effort. It just ends up in a fight anyway. Those people *will* be that way for the rest of their lives because they've issued instructions to themselves to stay precisely as they are.

We all have fixed mindsets. There's no way to get rid of them. But they become dangerous if they impede you from moving forward, doing the work you need to do to feel the way you want to feel. So, to solve for this, GOATs focus on generating *growth* mindsets.

If you recall, a fixed mindset person believes that intelligence is static, which leads them to …

- Avoid challenges
- Give up easily
- See effort as fruitless or worse
- Ignore helpful feedback, particularly negative feedback
- Ultimately feel threatened by the success of others

GOATs believe that intelligence can be developed. We're not just stuck with what we're born with: we can change at any age in any way we want.

A growth mindset pattern shows that intelligence can be developed and learned, which leads to desire to learn and a tendency to …

- Embrace new challenges and take risks
- Persist despite setbacks and tests that don't work
- See paths to mastery of skills necessary to improve their talents
- Learn from criticism through radical open-mindedness
- Find lessons and inspiration from others, applying these to themselves where they see fit

As a result, they achieve higher levels of income, happiness, and overall wealth and well-being.

When a GOAT wants something, they scan their mindsets to see if something they're thinking is stuck in the fixed-mindset rut. I got stuck in the "I have a bad memory" rut until I realized that I could train my brain to remember things better. That changed everything, and now I actually *do* remember more.

Growth-mindset GOATs look for something to learn in every-thing — from their work, clients, the world at large, and their own personal experiences. They are aware of others, and may even take advice from them if it's helpful. But they're never held back, worried that someone is going to take something away from them or prevent them from achieving their aims. The growth mindset protects them because everything is a learning experience. Every-thing offers them an opportunity to grow, and diverting around obstacles is one of their primary talents.

Your Dragon will giggle its pants off every time it throws an obstacle your way or reminds you of some made-up inner failing (fake news!). But GOATs see those challenges as ways to get better, become stronger, and share more of their methodologies with others so they, too, can overcome these problems. It completely backfires on the Dragon.

Job fulfillment has nothing to do with what you do, but rather how you think about it. In *The Happiness Advantage* by Shawn Achor, he often encourages his clients to rewrite their job descriptions into "calling descriptions." A janitor, he explains, can look at the mess he cleans up or his contribution to the health and wellness of the children at the school. This is called "job crafting." It's not about changing what you do, but how you think about it. Meaning and pleasure are not derived from what you do — you *create* the meaning. So, if you're determined to hate what you do and see no point to it, then you'll hate every Monday. You'll complain to your peers all day and live miserably.

The more you develop a strong growth mindset, the stronger your GOAT becomes, and the Dragon wins one less battle.

PERSONAL STANDARD OF EXCELLENCE

I do a lot of work with Realtors, as you know. I'd never become one. They work too many weird hours. But I respect them massively for what they do! That industry is known for being brutal for creating an environment of externalized goals. Every brokerage has different levels of achievement: Chairman's Club, Diamond, Platinum, and so on. These are levels set by the industry, and while some Realtors find them motivating, others get depressed at their inability to achieve them. If the desired level is missed, what follows is either disappointment or finding a way to game the system so they *do* achieve the desired level, albeit by cheating. GOATs live their lives with achievement blinders on — their blinders. They have no interest in what anyone else is doing because they figure that they're doing their own thing, and it has nothing to do with anyone else. They set their own standards of excellence, creating a set of rules and expectations that if consistently executed, generate precisely what they want, at a pace they can manage easily. External rewards and achievements are nice, but they're not the *point*.

In a world driven by arbitrary measuring sticks, rather than progress and practice, fear rules the day. We set a goal in January, then promptly freak out, worrying about how on earth we're going to achieve it. I've worked with people who've sold real estate for twenty-seven years, and every January is the same: they set a goal and promptly lose all confidence in their abilities. Worrying about goals typically leads to stagnation, paralysis, inconsistent behaviors, and worse. However, GOATs have an idea of what they want to make, what actions will get them there, what they'd do with the money, and just get to work.

They also have a clear idea of what it's all for. They're not doing anything that doesn't make a solid and material contribution to their lives, businesses, or relationships. This is yet another standard GOATs set: no busy work. Having set their own standards by which they want to live and interact with the world, it's simply a matter of showing up and doing the work.

One of my favorite examples is in Darren Hardy's book *The Compound Effect*. In one part, he talks about how he wanted to meet someone special. So, he sat down and wrote a ridiculously long description of her: hair color, where she was from, what she loved, how she loved, and so on. He wrote (so he says) forty pages of notes. But then he did something even more important: he wrote an *additional* forty pages on the changes he had to make in his own life to attract such a wondrous person. He set standards because, while he could not control when and how the woman in his life would appear, he could prepare himself to be instantly attractive when she did. It worked!

I did this in a much less voluminous way. After one failed marriage and another boob of a boyfriend, I decided I'd rather be alone than compromise my happiness for someone else. When Marc literally stumbled into my life, I felt an immediate "Well now, *that* looks delicious." Learning he'd injured his knee in a skiing accident, I naturally *had* to save him a seat near our boys' swimming lessons the next week so he could tell me all about it. He played "hangman" with my son and used the same word every week (Scooby Doo), pretending every time that he had no idea what word the proper answer was. He was financially self-sufficient. He rode motorcycles. He traveled. He had kids. And he was a happy person. Perfection!

I set standards for myself and for whom I wanted in my life, and I've got an incredible relationship. I set my standards for my business and how I wanted it to be run and how profitable it needed to be so I could do more fun things like trips to the Maldives and taking the kids to Italy. I set my own standards for the quality of my work, the type of clients I wanted, and the support team I have. I don't care about awards. I don't care about what other coaches are or are not doing. I don't care about the "Two Comma Club." Everyone else can do what they wish. I'm doing my thing, unapologetically and without compromise. That's GOAT living!

LIVING WITH PURPOSE ON PURPOSE

Mission statements are nice words in a picture frame on the wall that everyone nods at, memorizes, and then never thinks about again. You can kid yourself that sheer memorization or incantations of these statements are meaningful, but they're just words until you add emotion and personal commitments.

To get the life we want, we have to insert a little bit of planning. Planning is not goal-setting, so don't get them confused. Planning is simply adding intention to your dreams, with some account-ability and commitment thrown in to ensure it actually happens. I always say "deadlines are for doers" because getting things done typically requires us to put the commitment into our calendars. Carol Dweck neatly creates a particularly useful framework in *Mindset* to set these goals and milestones.

To know if you're living with purpose, think of something you want to do or know more about, or a problem that keeps popping up.

Then ask yourself the following questions:

1. *When* will you do it? Set the deadline!
2. *Where* will you do it? At home, the office, or somewhere else? Be incredibly specific.
3. *How* will you do it? What are the steps? Map them out. There might be two or there may be 200 but get them all down.

I then like to mix this in with one of my favorite phrases, which I heard from Brendon Burchard: "Courage or cowardice show up in the calendar."

Once they have their plan, the *when, where, and how*, GOATs put it in their planners, calendars, or wherever else they manage their commitments. They break it all down to the level of "I can do that" — and then get it done! Living with purpose includes being committed to yourself because without it, your plans are pointless and dreams turn to regrets.

The last step, to ensure you even take one, is to add in the whole reason you're doing this. In Book 3, we'll explore a specific strategy to do this, but for now, envision the thing you want to do or solve or learn and ask yourself, "Why is this important to me?" What will it add to your life or business? What's the point? GOATs thrive on having a point to everything they do. I've never met Elon Musk but I'd hazard a guess that every minute of his day has a point, even in his downtime. Purpose is the back-bone of feeding and tending your internal GOAT. It keeps you focused, energized, and motivated no matter what your Dragon or the universe throws your way.

DRIVEN BY HAPPINESS

I have a lot of phrases I like to throw around, and here's another one: *100% of happy people are successful, but only a fraction of successful people are happy.*

You can make all the money in the world, but without happiness, it's empty. Money with happiness, now that's way better! Sadly, few people take the time to figure out what makes them happy, and then wander around wondering why they hate their jobs, or why their relationships seem to always fizzle out.

People who live true GOAT lives can answer questions about what brings them joy on a dime, mostly because they're living that joy. I lived a miserable existence for a very long time. It was when I was closing down my agency, wanting to do something — anything — that would be more fulfilling that I figured out that performance coaching is what I wanted. Every day, I can't wait to get going. I'm excited about every opportunity to share my craft with people, leading them to their greatness.

Is something about your life not quite right? In *The Secret Letters of the Monk Who Sold His Ferrari*, Robin Sharma's character in the book feels that there was something wrong "with the texture of his life." He was moving ahead, charging really, without knowing why or thinking about whether this was the path he wanted to be on in the first place. It was head down, go to work, get it done, and hope your personal life doesn't explode (his nearly did). He was doing what he got promoted into, not what he loved to do. And once he started down that path, misery followed.

What would you say is the "texture" of your life? Is it smooth or abrasive? Is it ripped and torn, or smooth and shiny? A happy life never feels rough, unkind, or out of control. It doesn't feel directionless or pointless, but rather full, exciting, and meaningful. It is focused 100% on doing what makes you happy so your entire life, both personal and business, is so full of joy that you wonder at it daily. I do. Life can be hard, but it's never without a purpose and a plan.

There is no one definition of "happiness" because to each of us it means something different. In *The Happiness Advantage* by Shawn Achor, he states that scientists refer to happiness as "subjective well-being" because it's based on how we feel about our lives. Said another way:

> *Happiness is the experience of positive emotions — pleasure combined with deeper feelings of purpose and meaning.*

You can see that when GOATs combine purpose with a clear definition of happiness in their lives, with a plan on what to do, when and how, their overall universe becomes enchanting!

BE 1% BETTER

Cammy is one of my spitfire clients. I delighted in our calls because they were so full of updates, challenges, solutions, and commitments as to what she'd do next. She worked with a team of other high-powered real estate agents, but her time and attention were being dragged in a thousand directions. Something had to give, or she'd just give up.

But she was smart, taking things one small step at a time. First, she'd start with an app to help manage the zillions of calls she'd get every hour when a house went on the market. Agents were clamoring to see it, changing appointments, booking new ones, and so on. With up to ten new listings coming on at any time, this was nuts. But the app helped, and she freed up some time.

Then it was on to the next part: how could she stop fretting all night long? She couldn't sleep. She needed rest! So, we developed a routine of reviewing the day, and she kept a notebook handy all evening in case some new idea popped into her head. Her husband even got in on the deal! Then, each morning, she'd review her work and see if everything still had the same prioritization as the night before, book obligations and meetings in her calendar, and off she'd go! No worries. No sleeplessness. Pure control.

She never hit overwhelm because she measured out her steps into small, manageable, doable tasks. Some weeks, we focused on helping her communicate better with her husband. Other weeks, it was full-on wrestling a big business challenge to the ground. But the incremental steps led to a life and business that she hadn't seen before.

The idea of being 1% better comes from one of my favorite books, *Atomic Habits* by James Clear. There is so much packed into this book, but one lesson that has stayed with me and many others is the power of small steps. The British cycling team used to absolutely suck, so much so that companies would beg them *not to wear their stuff* because it was embarrassing. With a new GOAT-level coach, they brought in the concept of improving everything by 1%. After a few years of tweaking clothing material, the inte-rior of vans, the bikes, and the cyclists' sleeping habits (among many other things), they started winning — *really winning*. Olympic medals, world records, and more started piling up, and suddenly, they were the talk of the (cycling) town.

GOATs know that few things are accomplished with giant strides. The bigger the problem, the smaller the steps to be taken. This is when great care is needed; and so they go slowly, cautiously, and prudently to ensure the outcome is absolutely perfect.

Want to work out more consistently? *Start with push-ups, not a seven-day gym regimen.*

Want to be better at meeting deadlines? *Start with one small project and set a date of completion and a plan. Then put the steps in your calendar so you do them.*

Want to eat better? *Start with a snack a day that you convert into something better for you.*

GOATs don't make a ton of noise. They're the quiet ones at the back, not big on drawing attention because attention isn't the point. Feeling accomplished, and doing so in a way that makes them beyond thrilled to be alive, IS the point.

THE ONLY COMPETITOR IN THE ROOM

Leon has the confidence most people only wish they could muster. At my Mastermind, someone asked him if he'd grown up wealthy and privileged because surely his confidence stems from a life of getting everything he wanted. Knowing his story, I just whispered, "Whoa, boy" under my breath, but let him respond.

He shared his story with the group. He hadn't grown up rich or privileged. He was out the door at sixteen, having suffered terrible traumas, and was forced to constantly work through challenges just to get anywhere. Over time, this attitude leads him to help create a billion-dollar brokerage, which he eventually left to build another one (why not?!).

When he was done telling his story, the one prevailing thought he wanted the room to know was that he always assumed that he was the only competitor in the room. Sure, other people were around, but he figured he could always do better and just got to work.

And that last bit — the part where he "just got to work" — is one of the primary things that separates GOATs from Dragon-feeders. If you truly believe you are the only competitor in the room and focus on your own results and work, there can be no stopping you. Leon has a following because he's inventive, driven, and never sees any market or situation for which there isn't a unique approach.

He sees what everyone else is doing and typically goes in the opposite direction, mostly because everyone's just trying to imitate each other. Things must make sense for him to execute a single step. In real estate, newbies are encouraged to call their spheres and hump their way through the neighborhood. Just this past week, Leon explained how stupid that was: the newbie's sphere *knows* they're new! What you need is *their* network — the ones who aren't aware of how recently they got their license!

When you aren't worried about what or how anyone else is doing, life becomes incredibly simple. How do *you* measure progress for yourself? Leon hates goals. He doesn't want to *end* the game; he wants to *always be in it*. He measures progress by how much he has incrementally grown his business over a certain time period. Not enough? Turn up the gas. Doing great? Keep going! Seth Godin shares the story of Jones Soda in *Linchpin*. The business was valued at over $300 million at one point. None of this was achieved by doing what the industry was doing. The owner's words are clear. "I don't care what anybody does in the beverage industry. We've got to do what we've got to do. You have to know what they're doing, but you don't have to follow what they're doing."

GOATs see no need to compare themselves to others, nor do they play "follow the leader." They can take bits and pieces that work for them, but they discard more than they adopt. They read to learn and collaborate to hone their mental acuity, and then in Leon's words, "They just do the work."

FUELED — NOT FRIGHTENED — BY YOUR DARK SIDE

I have a dark side, and so do you. It's the yin to the "superpower" yang, the bright and awesome side, the part with massive talent. My dark side is the box I put myself into when I belonged to the church, living in constant fear of death and destruction, always full of guilt and shame. In my youth, I was bright and energetic and couldn't wait to take on the day. As I grew older with more and more rules to follow and guidelines to meet, my world got darker and darker.

A bird will sing when you first put it in a box, but eventually the darkness takes away its song. That was me. My absolute darkest moment was hanging upside down in my car, having rolled it down the embankment and then screeched across the pavement of that six-lane highway.

Dean Graziosi, real estate and coaching mogul, described an experience in his book, *Millionaire Success Habits*. When he was nine, he and his father, a contractor, slept in the bathroom of a home his father was remodeling. They had a space heater but no beds. When he looks back on those hard times, he reminds himself that the work he does now ensures he will *never* go back to that place again. And by "place," I don't mean that actual home; I mean the place of powerlessness, poverty, and helplessness.

In my dark place, I felt miserable, poor, and meaningless. Nothing I did felt fulfilling or right. Now, literally every single thing I do is predicated on three things: does it make me happy, wealthy, or fulfilled? If I cannot say a resounding "Heck yeah!" then I simply don't do the work. It's not for me. Typically, if I get a lackluster "maybe" in response to the question, I'm in peril of following after something or someone else. I'm imitating again. I'm pretending. I'm worried about money. And it's not my super-power, so I shouldn't be doing it.

GOATs know their dark side. They don't shy away from it or push it away. They accept it for what it is and use it as the fuel for their fire, what drives their days. It's a part of them, as much as their superpowers are a part of them.

FAILURE IS A COMPETITIVE ADVANTAGE

When Thomas Edison tried over 3,000 times to get light bulbs to work, he never looked at each successive "miss" as a failure. They just didn't work. Ray Dalio, hedge fund billionaire, challenges people to take his ideas, and pick them apart. Find the problem that he doesn't see. The feedback and discussions make his ideas stronger. Or he kills the plan. It's called "radical open-mindedness," and it's a concept I absolutely love.

I've tried countless things that haven't worked — five businesses, partnerships, friendships, business programs, strategies, ads. You name it, I've tried it, and most haven't worked. But the ones that *did* work, now those are special. Those I scaled up and made the focus of my life.

The word "failure" sounds like such an insult. Like Edison, GOATs change the phrase to "it didn't work," which is not in the least bit personal and allows you to move along to find the next thing that will! A slight change in mindset opens doors that appear shut but aren't locked. Anyone can walk through them.

Rejection is another form of failure made worse because it includes the judgment of others. Anyone in sales knows the sting of a sudden dial tone or a door slammed in the face. A meeting rescheduled over and over. So why don't GOATs get fazed by failure or rejection? What's their secret?

The answer is simple: they change how they explain the situation to themselves. GOATs look at situations as local and temporary. They know it won't be like this forever, that it will pass. GOATs aren't emotionally invested so that whether they fail or succeed, it doesn't reflect on them personally. It's just all part of the work they're doing! Dragon-feeders will take a negative view, saying, "This is horrible. It's never going to end. It's always going to be this way." GOATs move on. It's just testing.

If you really want a motivating book that kicks you into high gear at the same time, read *Winning* by Tim S. Grover. He talks about the tough times and challenges that break you down and make you tired. He calls these times your "greatest strength — your ticket out of hell." He goes on, "How do you get back to paradise after you've been through hell? You rebuild yourself into something stronger. Not the same as you were. Something stronger."

I read that passage over and over again. I've had my fair share of volcanic moments when things blow sky-high, shattering everything to bits. They cannot be rebuilt. Sometimes I leave the shards behind. But in all cases, if I look back on what I did with those experiences, I came out better, stronger, faster, and surer in my step. I rebuilt those friendships, businesses, and systems, and they were far better than what I'd started out with.

GOATs know this rebuilding process well. They welcome the tough times, the hard work, and the challenges that no one can seem to overcome. It gets their hearts racing, and they can't wait to get to it. Testing, learning, blowing things up, and rebuilding into something stronger is the name of the GOAT game, and one they play very well.

DO THE WORK MOST WON'T

There is no work that is "beneath" a GOAT. They're happy to do work that most people won't, but they don't care. If it gets the job done, then they do it. So many people want to act today as if they've been building a business or career for ten years. They resent the hard work, grunt work, and vociferously complain, but they lack the funds or abilities to do it any other way. You can't reap the rewards of a ten-year business or career before you've completed the first. Amazon, Google, and any great company started because the founders did the hard work, putting in the hours knowing that one day they'd reap massive benefits. If they'd been snobbish about the work, they would not be the legends that they are today.

Resentment against work can creep in at any stage, though. If your workplace grows and new faces start cropping up everywhere, you may feel like your influence has eroded. You don't have the face time with the boss that you once had. Those lunches and golf games whittle down from once a week to once a month. Work becomes irritating, and suddenly you don't want to do anything.

I've seen people go from a bitterness I could feel, to closing deals left and right because they pulled up their GOAT pants and changed how they looked at their situation. They finally realized that they would never get back what once was, so instead, they sought out work and even personal experiences that drove more happiness into their lives. The transformation was fast, and it was amazing to watch. Once again, it proved that happy people are the ones doing the hard work.

If you do the work no one will do for a time, you'll surpass those who disdain it in a hurry, moving on to the better things faster. Hard work is like working out, eating well, and meditating: it's 95% mental. Anyone can do the work when there's a clear process or a manual with instructions. Few people can be like Mark Cuban (massive brain crush), Serena Williams, Kobe Bryant, or Tom Brady. They put in the work when everyone went home. They changed their regimen when they had to but showed up at the right time. They did the work, over and over until it was perfect.

GOATs work on their mental game daily, picking up jobs no matter what they are because if it has to get done to achieve what they want, well then, their purpose is greater than their pride. They knuckle down, and get 'er done.

STAR CONNECTIONS

As GOATs do the work, get the results, and bring happiness along for the ride, they make sure that no one gets in their way. I call this having "Star Connections," and these are friends, teammates, employees, partners, and bosses that are aligned with their purpose and passions. When he had grown Amazon beyond his garage and the company was doubling at an insanely fast rate, Jeff Bezos would not budge on the people he'd hire. He had two things people had to be good at to get a job there: 1) make lists and 2) prioritize the list every day. The team was desperate for anyone with a pulse — anybody would work! But Jeff said no: if they didn't fit in immediately, what was the point? No one had time to train a newbie and get them up to the warp speed at which Amazon was moving. Hiring people who weren't absolutely perfect was beyond stupid; it was dangerous to the growth of the company. It would slow them down.

Whether you're adding people to your team, or new friends to your network, GOATs are absolutely ruthless in only letting people in that are already in line with their culture. They never settle for "close enough" or "we'll make it work." It's either perfect, or they keep looking. There is no settling and no compromising, either at work or in their relationships.

GOATs know that this is the key to compound growth. And if you noticed, Amazon hasn't done too badly.

NECESSARY ENDINGS

In the same way they begin carefully, GOATs know to end things when required too. Typically, you hire slow and fire fast, but the better process is to hire perfectly and fire with grace. The worst thing you could do is hold onto people — personally or professionally — who are dragging you down.

Necessary Endings by Dr. Henry Cloud has inspired me to gauge very carefully whether what I'm doing is working, or if it needs to end. It's not just firing people; it's ending business strategies that no longer work. In my case, it was partnerships that I had no business being a part of (even though I'd co-created them). I ended ad campaigns that weren't delivering results. I ended friendships that did nothing but make me sad and feel lost and confused. I ended a loveless marriage. I ended the stupid rebound boyfriend thing. I'm never ending my current marriage, though. Not a chance. That was the result of a Star Beginning, let me tell you!

GOATs are not afraid of the necessity to end things. They accept it as natural and not mean, as in the case of helping some-one find a place more suitable for their talents. You can hesitate to let people go from your life, imagining the person's loneliness, and feeling responsible for their reaction. GOATs know that how someone feels is not their responsibility, but ensuring that the ending is done with kindness and grace *is*. They know that some-times they don't get it right, but as with how they view failure, it's just testing. Something just doesn't work. It's not personal.

Later in this book, you'll find the exact strategy to end anything with grace, but with a swiftness that allows you to pivot and move on.

GOATs don't wait. Neither should you.

THE BODYMIND CONNECTION

We typically think about our bodies and minds as two separate things. But in *The Myth of Normal* by Gabor Maté, scientists are discovering that the two are so closely linked as to be inseparable, labelling it "bodymind" as one word, without spaces. This opens up more opportunities to use this bodymind connection to improve performance, health, and happiness.

As GOATs know to take care of their businesses from stem to stern, they *also* take care of their bodies. Nearly 40% of CEOs and other C-suite level execs have the physiques of professional athletes. They need to make sure they have the energy to do all the amazing things they want to do. They're driven, and they know they're likely the main reason other people move along. Without them, things slow down, and most GOATs don't like to go slower than they want.

Energy is self-generated. Caffeine helps, but when you need to make it through a tough work schedule, or a grueling week with the kids, you'll need more than just artificial substances to keep you going. All the energy, passion, and motivation you need you already have. You just have to learn how to tap into it.

Kim struggled with her health for a long time, but mostly because she wrestled with how she viewed herself. The world around her got all her attention and effort, and nothing was left for her. Her health took a back seat to everything, and she started to physically fall apart. There came a time when that had to stop. Through a valiant effort of will and purpose, she started to change the trajectory of her life. She had work to do, so she had to have the energy to do it! She'd already doubled her income working with me; but FFS, she was NOT done, ladies and gentlemen! She got a knee brace, lost weight, and engaged her fellow master minders in supporting her to help her stay accountable. She showed up. She did the work. And the results are paying off.

When you want to do things like never before, you have to take care of yourself like never before too. Eat well. Get sleep. Move in any way you can. If this is new, start tiny. One push-up. A single good snack. One minute of meditation or deep breathing. A slight change to your evening or morning routine. All of these and more will create the environment to succeed.

GOATs are aware that when they are truly in tune with their bodies, they start generating whatever sensations or feelings they need. If they are feeling down, they know how to make themselves feel better. If they need support or comfort, or are feeling lost, they have ways to take control and do something to mitigate or process the feeling. If they're insecure about doing something new, they can find the trigger to get them to move in the direction of what scares them, knowing that confidence and motivation will follow. The solutions to all of this and more are coming up, but stay with me. There's more GOAT-ness for you to discover.

DOWNTIME IS HIGHLY VALUED

A GOAT is constantly coming up with new ideas on how to get the most out of life, but not always using conventional methods. In circumstances that aren't clear, or when the solution is not immediately forthcoming, they have a process whereby they can simply wait for the answer to arrive, without forcing it to come to the surface. It can be done in many ways and goes by many names:

- Thinking time
- Downtime
- Personal time
- Self-care

I love the "thinking time" reference because that's precisely what needs to happen to generate big ideas. The idea comes from the book, *The Road Less Stupid*, in which Keith J. Cunningham goes through an exceptionally elaborate process to still his mind and think about something — a problem, challenge, new idea, and so on. I won't go into the steps (there are fifteen), but the idea is sound: no matter how long or fancy the process gets, you take time regularly out of your week to do nothing but think.

I was behind in getting topics to organizers for a conference in March this past year, and I started to panic. It was January; they needed my topics for the schedule, and I was drawing a massive blank. Every time I tried to think, I felt nothing but mental constipation. So, I stopped forcing my brain to come up with something interesting. I put a fresh page of my giant sticky paper on the wall, put up my feet, and stared at the blank sheet of paper. I let my mind drift, finding meandering paths and questions: what were my clients struggling with? What big "AHAs" did we generate and what was it about? In about twenty minutes, I had nine topics from which the conference organizers chose three.

Forcing thoughts is like forcing success: it cannot be done, certainly not well or without pain. The best ideas come when you give your brain some rest. GOATs do this constantly. They take breaks. They read to find new ideas. They meditate. GOATs get a bad rap because people make the assumption that they are working like psychos and never see their families. But the opposite is most often true (unless they don't want it to be, and that's a choice too). When your brain has no chaos, the best ideas effortlessly come through.

Sometimes, to get clarity on what to do next, or to get inspired on something new and exciting, you have to remove yourself entirely from your business. I've had clients take off to Puerto Rico, Europe, Florida, and a cottage in the woods just to get away from their busy lives. This time away allows your brain to become calm, allowing your greatness to flow more freely. We can get all gummed up mentally when there's too much going on. GOATs take this time to unwind, relax, let the brain just chill out for a bit, knowing that when they return, they'll be in top form.

BE INTENTIONAL WITH YOUR TIME

When people think about being productive, they often confuse it with being "busy." Being productive has everything to do with being intentional with your time. If you look at a GOAT's calendar, it's got a nice mishmash of meetings, creative time, family time, and whatever else is important to them. It's mapped out, so that when they're at work, that's their focus, and vice versa at home. They don't over-time block, allowing for some flexibility in their schedule, but making sure that the important work gets done.

They plan their days the night before (or even the week before or on Sundays) to minimize unpleasant surprises and emergencies. When they are with family, they don't think about work. The same is true when they are working — they don't feel guilty about neglecting their family because they are not. Everyone gets their undivided attention. They make this work by managing their time with the greatest of care. GOATs also train the people around them to respect their time. If they're going to get back to the family on time, they need to be focused on work. This means their kids or spouses can't call them every second of the day. Getting dragged away by "gotta minute meetings" at the office slows them down, so they put mechanisms in place to have other people answer questions, or systems by which people can get the support they need without depending solely on them.

Heather's husband loved talking with her. It was sweet, except he had horrible timing: he always wanted to chat during her most productive time in the morning. His job took him away primarily in the afternoon. So, every morning, he'd wander down to her office, sit on the stairs beside her, and shoot the breeze. That didn't work for her, putting her further and further behind. In trying to be polite and talking with him, her business suffered. So, one day she asked him if there was a better time to chat that didn't infringe on her workday. He was more than happy to oblige!

Turns out that people are three times more likely to say *yes* than you think, so go ahead and ask for space and privacy. GOATs tell people every day what time they have, putting people into their schedule so that when that time comes, they have their undivided attention. This is respect. It's also showing your greatness. So feel free to train your family to respect your time and avoid calling you at deep-work times so you can focus on them when you're at home. Find solutions at work to avoid being distracted when you're with your friends and family, so you're not called away at dinner or special moments you don't want to miss.

GOATs get it: their time is everything. It's the only resource that will never, ever renew, and they want to make the most out of every minute.

ARE YOU LIVING YOUR GOAT LIFE?

Seth Godin states, "You don't' need more genius — you need less resistance," and he's 100% correct. To live a GOAT life, you need to stop resisting, start asking for what you want and need, and then get to work. You stop settling and become relentless in your desire for the greatest life, business, careers, and relationships of all time. They are yours for the taking. Now let's figure out how to get it done.

BOOK 2

HOW TO SHRINK YOUR DRAGON

I could have ended the book right here, leaving you with an explanation of the phenomena of the two warring forces that continuously fight for your attention, but that would not be helpful. Instead, the rest of this book is dedicated to showing you precisely *how* to make changes to living your life — both in the real world and the one inside your head — so you can become the happiest, wealthiest, and most fulfilled version of yourself. You can live your sweet GOAT life, without the distraction of a hollering, blood-sucking, venom-spewing Dragon.

Your "homework" is to do something — anything. Pick one strategy and try it out for at least a week. Make the steps small to the point where, when you look at the effort and time required or the magnitude of the adjustments, you can say to yourself, "*I can do that.*" I call this "little chunking," the process of de-magnifying something that feels so unattainably huge into a little task that almost feels so small it's cheating. It's not. It's progress.

You will not be perfect at this. If you're struggling with being inconsistent at applying these new strategies, start with naming and *claiming* your emotions — the first strategy in the How to Shrink Your Dragon section!

We have amazing and infinitely plastic brains. We can change how we think, act, and believe at any time in our lives. I encourage you to set aside any previous defeat at attempting these strategies (or ones like them). Perhaps you didn't see the point of meditation before. You may have told yourself, "I suck at meditation. It never works for me" in your most fixed-mindset inner voice. Or perhaps you misunderstood *how* it's done, trying to follow what everyone else was doing instead of adapting the practice to fit *your* brain. I give you permission to adapt any strategy to your preferences from hereon in.

The most important approach to take for the rest of this book is this:

I will adopt the strategies that work for my brain and my GOAT and evolve them to the point where they are an integral part of my life.

You don't have to do them all. I don't care if you meditate for three breaths or two hours. It's all still "meditation," so do what works for you. Hate time blocking? Find a different way to organize what you do! Feel under pressure to have the "miracle morning" routine or you struggle to join the 5:00 am club? Make your own miracles and invite yourself and your GOAT to your *own* morning routines! And literally screw the rest. How other people do things is how other people do things. They're not you, so stop trying to be them. Your GOAT life awaits; and the sooner you can shut up that Dragon, the faster your GOAT can dance and bleat its way into your day. And you won't help your GOAT by tending to someone else's! Feed your own!

Let's begin now with shrinking your Dragon. Sayonara, sucker.

Your days are numbered.

HOW TO SHRINK YOUR DRAGON

You cannot slay the nasty Dragon in your head because it still controls your breathing and heartbeat and some other rather essential functions. Fear still has a place in our lives but not as a barrier to our greatness. You *can* shrink it, however, to regain full control of your ability to think, create, problem solve, and build fulfilling, beautiful relationships, businesses, and careers. So, no slaying today. Just shrinking.

It's not a matter of training your Dragon, either. I loved that movie, but training a Dragon harnesses its power to be used by you. Problem is, the Dragon I'm talking about is unkind, doesn't play well with others, is sneaky, and prohibits you from actually being awesome. So, no training of Dragons either.

What's next are strategies clinically or otherwise proven to physically shrink your amygdala, avoiding the hijack situations where all rational thought flees the building. We replace those reactions with a firm sense of control. Studies have shown that in only eight weeks, if you can implement some of these regular practices — or even *one of these practices* — you can shrink the physical size of the amygdala. It amazed me that these changes could appear so quickly. After a lifetime of struggle, fear, anxiety, anger, and other emotions I can't even name, it has been one of the most heartening experiences to discover that peace and control are so close at hand.

You just have to do it.

All self-help books motivate. But if you read them carefully, they are literally *begging* people to implement their ideas and not just put the book down and carry on with life.

I'm going to join the line: do the work. Anything you can. I have a podcast I want to start that is dedicated to getting people to *do work*, not sit on the fence or tell me, "You're right." I despise that phrase because the person is not saying that they believe me; they are just telling me that I'm correct without taking responsibility to do something with it.

So, remove "you're right" from your vocabulary as you read this. Change it to "that's right, and here's what I'm going to do about it," and you, my friend, are off to the Dragon-shrinking races

NAMING AND CLAIMING YOUR EMOTIONS

Few people chomp at the bit to get into their feelings. This is one of my least favorite exercises as an autistic woman, with traumas in my past that caused me to clam up. I experience life but struggle to *feel* it. But I've paid a hefty price for that. When I was in my twenties and even into my thirties, I would fly into rages or filibuster for hours. Most times, mid-speech, there would be a tiny voice inside my head saying, "*This is kinda overdoing it, don't you think?*" I ignored that voice because I didn't know how to regain control of my emotions. They just ran amok, and God help whoever was in the way. Those moments did not make me proud. And while I don't cringe about them anymore, they are a cautionary tale I remind myself about every so often. My relationships are important to me. I don't want any stubbornness about not wanting to "feel" life get in the way or wreck them.

When it comes to emotions, one of our greatest challenges is to name them. If you cannot name what you feel, your brain will be unable to process and deal with it. Most of us can come up with three basic descriptions for how we feel:

- Mad
- Sad
- Happy

As I continued the research for this book, I discovered Emotion Wheels. These are lists of emotions by various names and intensities, categorized starting with broad feelings like "angry" or "sad" or "happy." As you go further out, they become more specific, ranging into words like "dismayed" and "inferior" or "energized." There are literally hundreds of these online, and I encourage you to find the one with the most relatable words for you. Here's the one that I have been using. You can download this one at www.dragonandgoatbook.com.

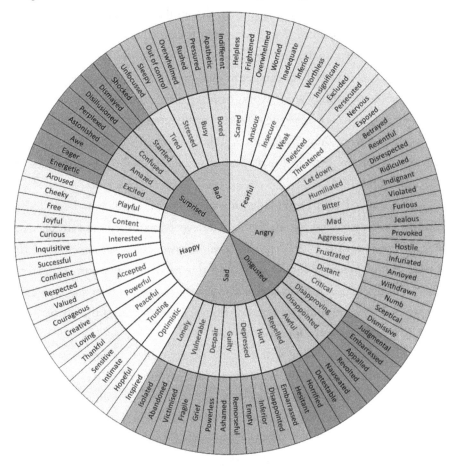

To use the wheel, simply ask yourself this question: "How do I feel about __?" Yourself, your work, a relationship, or life in general, it doesn't really matter. I do what I call a "break check" several times a day as I continue to train myself to feel more of life, so it's not always about something specific. Then you simply go through the wheel and write down any words that pop out at you. For words that you're not sure of, write them down anyway. It doesn't matter if you start at the outside edges and the most specific words and work toward the broader terms, or the other way around. Remember, you adapt this process to *you*. I'm just giving you the tools to begin.

Get out your GOAT-book and write down any and all words that stand out. You will find that sometimes you have contradicting feelings. You can be tired but energized, excited and annoyed, thankful and bitter. Notice in particular the positive emotions. We're not wired for positivity. We're wired to run away from dragons, tigers, and bears. It worked brilliantly thousands of years ago, but today this negativity can get in our way. The tendency to see the scary things, the reason things won't work, or imagining some sort of horrible outcome to our actions is one of the most powerful deterrents to living the GOAT life. It's one of your Dragon's favorites. Take a moment to recognize that good feelings can pop up, even in the darkest of situations or the most troublesome of relationships.

When I talked with Dr. Hendry, my psychologist, about how I was feeling seriously conflicted about my son going to university, she asked me a simple question, *"Why isn't it okay to feel both good and bad emotions at the same time?"* This woman stumps me on a regular basis, and this particular question stopped me dead. I had thought that I had to feel all one way or another. Not so, apparently. You can and *will* feel multiple types of things, and sometimes they won't make sense. They're not always supposed to.

When you see the list of words, start asking yourself where those feelings might be coming from. My son went to his first year of university with his best buddy. They were going to work side by side in mechanical engineering at a school five hours away from where I live. There was great joy in watching them go off together. I felt hopeful, proud, and awesome. But halfway through the year, his buddy realized that engineering was *not* his calling, and he dropped out.

My son tried switching schools to be closer to home, but it didn't work. This year he's off to school alone, not knowing a soul because his first year was entirely online due to the pandemic, and everything was closed. My feelings were very, very mixed. I was proud of him for doing such a hard thing. I was excited for his prospects, not relying on his friend network as much, meeting new people, seeing his potential play out. But as I went around the Wheel, I found the word "annoyed" popping out. That surprised me. What was that all about?

I realized that despite knowing that his buddy needed to find a new path and being excited for him in this discovery, I was still annoyed at the situation. And that's okay, Dr. Hendry was saying. I had to repeat those words to myself over and over. As I write this book, I've just dropped him off to begin his new adventure. I don't know how it's going to go, but I do know how to ensure that my anxiety or worry about his development this year won't destroy my peace. He's got this. Everything is going to be okay.

One of my clients is using an app to get her health back in order. Just this morning, she sent me a text with a synopsis of what the app observed from her behavior this past week. It describes perfectly what we're trying to do here with emotions, and why it's such an important exercise:

"If you've found yourself feeling suddenly overwhelmed by emotion, it can be incredibly helpful to pause and examine the emotion. When we do this, it's important to practice non-judgment and empathy for your-self; beating yourself up for feeling what you feel is usually counterproductive. If you're able, put a name to the emotion and then see if you can break it down a little. Ask some "who, what, where, when, and why" questions: Where did this feeling come from? Is there any sort of a primary emotion — an emotion beneath the one that has manifested that is really the problem — that you need to address first? Is this emotion being brought on by a specific person, place or thing? Not only does this process help reveal the validity and intricacies of the emotion you're feeling, but going through these questions may just redirect your attention enough to lessen the intensity of the emotion itself." [7]

---

7   The app is called "Reframe."

People who regulate their emotions by naming, processing, and accepting them see huge advantages in their lives, including but not limited to:

- An improved ability to handle stress
- Better at dealing with conflict with more grace and better outcomes
- Improved stability — both mental and emotional
- Ability to meet long-term goals
- Less friction as they progress through life
- Ability to handle challenges without running away or being overwhelmed
- Improved overall health, mentally, physically, and spiritually

The more work you do on naming and processing how you feel, the more stable you will become. Do not try to push your feelings away. I've done that for years, and am paying a hefty price.

It doesn't work anyway. They build up, and at some point, you blow. Worse, emotions with nowhere to go turn to self-hatred. As you do this emotion work, chances of explosions and outbursts go way, way down and you begin to repair your opinion of yourself. Some of my clients are frustrated because they cry at the drop of a hat. By working on what drives that reaction, they've been able to stop and behave as the best version of themselves for any situation. Like them, you'll be able to choose how you want to feel ahead of time, or react with a steady mind.

Here's a quick summary to help.

1. Think of something you'd like to explore emotionally. It could be how you feel about yourself, your work, your future, your kids, spouse, friends, etc.
2. Go through the Emotion Wheel and write down any and all words that pop out. Not sure? Write it down and put a question mark beside it.
3. Test the emotions with "who, what, where, when, and how" questions. Be careful with asking "why," as those questions can sometimes turn into self-berating. Is there anything deeper, beyond the initial feelings?
4. Accept the emotions for what they are.

5. Notice the contradictions and accept that you're allowed to be conflicted. It's part of the human experience.

6. Also notice the positive emotions. Train your brain to see the good in the world, and within you. We're not wired for it, so we have to train ourselves into it!

7. Repeat this process daily.

As you practice naming your emotions, you'll find that when a big feeling strikes — especially from the "big four," anger, aggression, anxiety, and fear — you'll be able to recognize the sensation and use tools to de-stress or de-magnify the situation.

If you want a life that never feels emotionally out of control, opportunity awaits. Get a copy of the Emotion Wheel at www.dragonandgoat book.com. But remember, there are zillions out there. Pick the one that works best for you.

Just do it.

PROCESSING THE PHYSICAL ENERGY OF EMOTIONS

Emotional moments are like waves, building to a crescendo. Naming and claiming the emotions will lessen the severity of these waves, but it's not quite enough to fully dissipate the feelings. Our bodies and minds are intertwined and often, even before we acknowledge that we're having an emotional reaction, our bodies have felt the impact. Sweaty palms, tight throats, beating hearts, and muscle tension are just some of the symptoms that we physically feel when we're in the throes of a situation. Giving words to our feelings will get us under control, but to complete the process we have to physically dispense of the emotional energy.

Dr. Hendry asked me what happens when I get really angry — when I don't throttle it back and stuff it away. "Things break," I replied. "Great," she said. I looked at her like puppies do when they hear a funny sound, head cocked to the side, blank stare. "Good?" I asked. I used to get in trouble when my rage led to destruction, not a high five. She wondered if there were other things I might do, things I could break or attempt to destroy, that I wouldn't regret later. My punching bag came to mind, and while I can't punch it (It's too hard and my autism makes physical pain truly debilitating), I can take a baseball bat to it! Ha! I had an outlet for all my rage, in a way that allows the emotions to complete their process through my body.

The beauty of completing the cycle and allowing our feelings to integrate within us, becoming useful tools instead of crippling barriers, is that it brings us to logic, rational thought, and our true creative genius. The end of the wave comes when we are physically free of our emotions, and once we achieve that wondrous status, we can think clearly, do the right thing, and get back to life.

Physically processing emotions can take whatever form you want. The only rule is safety, for you and for others. It bears mentioning that your physical emotional energy should never be transferred to another human being. Talk with your family, friends, or colleagues about what you're going to do so they can see it as healthy, not a reason to call the authorities.

So what can you do? Here are some ideas, but feel free to find your own opportunities!

- Punch a punching bag
- Rip paper to tiny shreds
- Throw rocks at a fence
- Punch a pillow
- Scream into a pillow
- Do push-ups, burpees, or any physically taxing and quick-moving exercise
- Run in place
- Pump your arms
- Cry your heart out — like *really* cry

Let the wave of emotions flow naturally from you, not because you are trying to rid yourself of these important feelings. Rather, it's so you teach yourself that emotions are a natural part of a good, fulfilling life and can be useful to you. Anger ensures you stand up for yourself. Guilt and shame can help you look back on how you handled a situation and find ways to be a better person, or improve your interactions. Sadness allows us to feel grief and pain without it turning into resentment or suffering. But these strong emotions cannot be our allies if we stuff them away, holding them in instead of giving them due process.

REGULAR MINDFULNESS MEDITATION

Have you ever watched the show *Billions*? I love that show, and not just because one of the main characters is a high-performance coach like me. What intrigues me is that this high-powered, high-stress moving and shaking hedge fund had a dedicated meditation room. This got me thinking: why would they do that? Everyone is moving at a hundred miles an hour, and yet they take time to meditate. My clients, who do *not* run billion-dollar funds, constantly complain that they "don't have the time" to meditate, or claim it "doesn't work for them." So what gives?

Turns out *most* billionaires meditate. Bill Gates, the late Steve Jobs, Salesforce CEO Marc Benioff, and the legendary hedge fund billionaire Ray Dalio all take time out for mental quiet. Dalio even stated that meditation was the single most important reason for his incredible track record of success.

I'm not saying that meditation leads to being a billionaire, but I do run my business by looking at what those big guns are doing and following suit. They don't endlessly take classes or go to conferences. They attend few networking functions. They read, and they meditate. And then they do epic work.

I've got the reading thing down pat. I'd already been reading since childhood, so reading business-related books as fodder for my own private practice made oodles of sense. Meditation however, well, that would take more work. I didn't have a regular practice. It felt way too "woo-woo," and I didn't see the point. And if I don't see a point, my brain just shuts off and moves on.

I would be a multi-millionaire if I took a penny for the number of times I've heard, "Meditation doesn't work for me," mostly because I'd take those pennies from myself. I've always claimed that I was too busy, can't sit still, I forget, and so on. I have 180 screens in my head, and they're all on!

However, I've discovered that combined with emotional regulation, meditation is the single most powerful practice for living our greatest lives. So how could I make this work for me with a lifetime's worth of "I can't do it" in my veins? First, I had to under-stand the science. If there was logic, I was in. I came across two incredible articles that detailed the powerful results from regular meditation practice. The first, from Harvard, states:

> *"Our results suggest that meditation can produce experience-based structural alterations in the brain. We also found evidence that meditation may slow down the age-related atrophy of certain areas of the brain."* [8]

The second article goes even further: They found that as little as eight weeks of consistent mindfulness practice is enough to tame and shrink your amygdala. What's more, [Lazar's] research shows that amygdala taming correlates with changes in stress: "The more stress reduction people reported, the smaller the amygdala got." [9] If meditation is the ticket to a shrunken Dragon and can slow down age-related atrophy and change how I react to stress, this girl is *in!* The next challenge for me now that I knew my lifetime of stress reactions could be abated in eight weeks of "regular" practice, was to figure out what "regular" or "consistent" means. They are subjective terms.

The answer came as I was waiting my turn to speak at a conference recently. The woman before me, Anusha Wijeyakumar, was an expert on meditation practices, using them to help newly diagnosed breast cancer patients deal with the pain, the process of chemotherapy, and more. I admired her not only for having zero slides to guide her thoughts (Ninja move!), but also for the straightforward way she described how we all have access to the ability to meditate.

Her presentation, published in a book called *Meditation with Intention*, is all about five-minute meditations. Over and over, she told the group, "We all have five minutes." There is no excuse in the world we can come up with to say we don't.

Meditation is best done first thing in the morning when our brains are the most receptive to positive information. But if you can't swing it first thing, then literally any time in your day counts. In case your Dragon is screaming its fool

---

8   https://scholar.harvard.edu/sara_lazar/home (11) Amygdala activation

9   https://motherhoodcommunity.com/feeling-impulsive-or-overly-emotional-here- are-3-proven-ways-to-calm-down-an-overactive-amygdala/

head off right now about how you can't do this, let me give you places and situations where you can meditate for five minutes:

- In your (parked!) car or home office
- Before you greet your family and begin personal time
- Waiting to pick up the kids from school
- As soon as you wake up, before you get out of bed
- Right before you go to sleep
- At the gym, right before or after exercise
- While walking the dog (walking meditations count too!)
- While waiting for dinner to cook in the oven

And while meditation experts recommend you sit while doing so, the most important thing is *doing it*. So, however you get it in, go for it. Walking, sitting, lying down — who cares *how* you do it? The important thing is to get past what's obstructing the practice and get to it. When I gave myself permission to lie down while meditating, it changed everything. I may one day sit in a chair; but for now, I get the most out of chilling in a supine position, first thing in the morning.

Think of the excuses you've given yourself *not* to meditate. Are they valid? Can you switch them around to something that works for you? Did someone tell you that unless you did it "their way," you were "doing it wrong"? Ignore those voices. Your Dragon put them up to it. Instead, evolve the practice to a time that works for you.

Before we continue, a short word on "regular" and "consistent." I had a client who week after week, argued with me about her incapability of being "consistent" with her time management processes. Finally, one day, I asked her what was truly going on. Why was she so frustrated and adamant that she couldn't be consistent?

She explained that she equated "consistent" with "daily," and what I was asking her to do was something that was nearly *impossible* to do daily! Be careful about the associations and definitions you give to certain things like "consistency" and being "regular." It can be once a week, twice a month, once a year, and so on. In the case of meditation, it is *best* to do it daily, but it doesn't have to be at the same *time* or *place* every day.

If you're a real meditation hold-out and refuse to see how five minutes of meditation could ever work for you, let me ask you this: Can you take three deep breaths? If you just stop in your day and take those three breaths, they can have the equivalent effect of two hours of meditation.

I love to combine the Emotion Wheel work with meditation. It adds a depth to the practice and encourages me to access and accept how I feel. I highly recommend you do this too, combining the processes of naming and taming emotions *and* quietly bringing your thoughts to a place of peace.

So there, you *can* meditate. Now go figure out exactly what type, time, style, sitting or lying position works for you and stick that in your calendar. Ommmmmmmm …

SELF-WORTH AND THE ROOT OF INCONSISTENCY

A few months ago, I got sick of a few of my clients telling me they either completely avoided the work they were supposed to do or were inconsistent with their practice. Being me, I decided to dive into the research behind such behavior. What I found stunned me. The reason people are inconsistent, avoid things, or procrastinate has nothing to do with their time management skills and *everything* to do with one single thing: their level of self-com-passion and *self-worth*.

Think about it. If you tell yourself that you can't do something, aren't worthy, smart enough, capable, or whatever nonsense story you cook up, you crucify your self-worth. Holding onto anger and pain converts to self-hatred, pushing you deeper into that hole. It's impossible to do the hard work if your emotions are stuck in inferiority, inadequacy, or worthlessness. It makes sense that when you feel this way, you will avoid the important GOAT work, and your Dragon helpfully shows you alternatives that are less difficult or scary.

If you are avoiding your GOAT-work, there's a misfire in how you view yourself or your ability to complete that work. This is where you go through that Emotion Wheel again and ask yourself with brutal honesty, "How do I really feel about myself?" Listen to the answers that come up. There's a message in there for you. You can be consistent at anything with the right self-worth.

Staying consistent requires setting the frequency of how you want to be regular at a level you can manage. Whether it's daily, hourly, monthly, quarterly, annually, or once every ten years, choose an interval you can manage without stress, becoming overwhelmed, or taking on too much. Don't be a hero. You're useless if you burn out. Adjust the work schedule and timing to the way your brain likes it best. Give don't care how anyone else does their work, how long they "time block," or how often they do it. The focus is 100% on you and your best path forward.

One last time: inconsistency, avoidance, and procrastination are all rooted in you feeling badly about yourself or your work. And it's 100% solvable. Now go do the Emotion Wheel and close the gap between how you feel now and your GOAT level of self-appreciation and self-love!

BREATHING DEEPLY

Deep breathing has been like meditation for me: I struggled to see the point of it. I know it's supposed to calm you down, add oxygen to the body, blah blah blah. But beyond that, I couldn't really see its ongoing value. Sure, it helps calm my nerves before I go on stage, but I don't do that every day.

Turns out, breath work is as essential as meditation, which in itself is as essential for emotional regulation. They're all deeply, deeply connected, which is why meditation always incorporates it.

Engaging in regular, intentional, and conscious breathing is an anti-anxiety technique. When you focus on your breath, you can *only* be where you are in that very moment. Anxiety is unnecessary worry about a future you haven't yet lived. It's pointless and yet massively addictive. We try to predict what will happen, and in so doing, we come to believe that it is true *right now.* That sounds insane, but it's precisely how our brains are wired. Thoughts, thought often enough, become what we believe. If you think that catastrophe is around every corner, you bring massive anxiety right to your door. Breathing eliminates that panic, because it brings you back to what's right in front of you — what is real, tangible, and true. It will also accomplish any of the following:

- Reduce stress
- Create feelings of openness
- Generate more love to yourself and others

- Increase gratitude
- Generate clarity
- Improve your ability to communicate so you can get more of what you want
- Strengthen connections

In my high-performance certification training, we did an exercise that I absolutely love called "Release Tension/Set Intention." This is a two-minute exercise, but in a pinch, you can do it in one minute (so no "I don't have time" self-talk). It's intended to ensure you don't drag stress and overwhelm through your day. At each transition — going from home to work or back again, from a meeting to doing work, from lunch to whatever comes next — you go through this exercise. In so doing, you release the brain's habit of holding onto stress or going through its rumination process and point your brain toward what lies ahead.

Here's how it works:

Step 1: Release tension

For one minute, you simply sit (lie, stand on your head, it doesn't matter) and breathe deeply. While breathing, say the word, "release." This tells your brain you want to stop thinking about whatever you just finished doing because you're needed at full capacity for what comes next. It releases your brain from being distracted and guides it to the present moment and out of the past or future.

Step 2: Set intention

The second minute is where you visualize doing the thing that comes next. If you're going home and you have kids, you can visualize how you'd be your *best* parent. How would you talk to them? How would you behave? What would you ask? Where would you put your phone and how would you proceed through the evening? Get right in there! Build a credible and clear picture. As you continue to breathe, you tell your brain precisely how it should act, and because your thoughts lead to your behavior, you actually *do* behave that way.

Breathing brings you out of the past and back from the unknowable future into the moment in which you are, right now. The instruction to release attention or tension from the previous situation helps the process. Clearly identifying how you want to be and interact with people on what comes next issues instructions to the brain on how to be in the present moment. You'll find that by the end of the day, you don't feel overwhelmed, stressed, or fatigued. You stop dragging your baggage through the day.

Like me, I hope you now see the point if you hadn't before. You *can* meditate, and you *can* practice deep breathing. Together, they are Dragon-shrinking powerhouses! You breathe all day; I'm just asking you to be more intentional with it! The more consistently you practice these two methodologies, the smaller your amygdala will become, and the less power your anxiety, fear, and anger will have on your life. You will always have emotional experiences, but you'll be able to handle the wave and stay in control of yourself. Remember, do it every day for five minutes, and after eight weeks, you'll start to see that life is not as frustrating or overwhelming as you thought!

GRATITUDE AND APPRECIATION

Here's another Dragon-Shrinking quickie: Did you know that the simple act of showing gratitude and appreciation can shrink the size of your amygdala? That Dragon of yours does *not* like being grateful. It prefers entitlement, so you can imagine how much it will fight you on this one.

It really doesn't matter how you decide to show gratitude or appreciation; what matters is that you do it. You can keep it quietly to yourself in a journal. Or you can message or call someone to overtly show how much they mean to you or thank them for the support they've given. Journaling didn't work for me, because all I could think of was "ditto" from what I'd been grateful for the day before. But challenging myself to find something I can thank someone for as a daily task got my brain really thinking. I can't send the same person the same text every day. I had to be inventive! When you teach your brain to look around and show true and real appreciation, it begins to see even more awesome and gratitude-worthy things around you.

One cautionary note: Don't do this without the intention, because it won't have the Dragon-shrinking effect you're looking for. This isn't something you just mindlessly check off every day. If you're not truly thankful, you're going to sound like an ass.

People sometimes get appreciation and gratitude mixed up with recognition. They are not the same. Recognition is appreciation publicly stated to others. Sadly, companies equate doing a roll call at an office meeting as having the same value as showing authentic appreciation. It's not even close! Gratitude is heartfelt. Recognition can be emotionless.

Here's the good news if you have been practicing recognition but maybe not getting the appreciation part right. In Gary Chap-man's sister book to *The 5 Love Languages, called The 5 Languages of Appreciation in the Workplace,* he goes into great detail about how to properly appreciate people. Spoiler alert: there are really only four languages of appreciation in the workplace, since "physical touch" can lead to jail time, not a promotion. The four that work in the workplace include:

- Quality Time
- Words of Affirmation
- Acts of Service
- Gifts

He explains that unless you train your brain properly, you will always appreciate others in *your* language, not theirs. My primary language of appreciation is "acts of service," so if you help me out, I love you to death! I'm busy. I need help. Jen on my team is the absolute opposite. She's more of a "get outta here, I got this!" kind of person. Her main language is "gifts," which unfortunately happens to be my *least* powerful language.

But before we go on to how I bridged that gap, it's important to note that each language has several sub-languages. If your primary language is "words of affirmation," you may not like it done in front of people. Or you may love it when it's shouted from the rooftops! You may prefer certain kinds of words or situations, times when you are most receptive to the appreciation being shown. So not only do we need to learn the languages of those we wish to appreciate, but we also need to be careful to understand the nuances of the main languages as well.

I had to ask Jen to help me out because I grew up with a ton of expensive stuff, but I could also see how these material things didn't mean much when other parts of the relationships weren't healthy. You can't give someone flowers when all they want is your time. You can't pat someone on the back when what they really need is a helping hand. In Jen's case, I had zero idea of the type or style of gift that would be truly meaningful. I needed her help. Turns out her most appreciated gift is financial, but with the stipulation that it had to be used only for her and for what brings her joy.

Now every year, when I want to show her my deep appreciation for working with me, I know precisely the type of gift to give and when she'll appreciate it most. I try to use her primary and secondary languages as often as I can, and she reciprocates. When you have this level of understanding of how someone wants to be appreciated and recognized, you get more out of it.

If you are interested in finding your language of appreciation, just go to www.mbainventory.com. If you have a team, send everyone to it! Leaders get a full report of everyone's languages so that the next time they talk with each person, they can do it properly and really let their gratitude land.

Dragons hate everything about this process, which is why it's so important to take the time and at least find out your own language, either by reading the book or taking the inventory test (or both). It's been invaluable to me and to the clients who have taken this to heart. Production skyrockets, and people feel truly seen and valued. If you want your team to produce at higher performing levels, making them feel valued is the key. If you want to be a better leader, you need to get people to follow you not because they have to, but because they want to.

THE STORY CHANGING PROCESS

When you research "how to live a more fulfilled life" or dig into meditation, a lot of what is talked about revolves around our thoughts. And as you saw in Book 1, thoughts are fed by emotions, and this combination builds our belief systems, which in turn drives what we do.

It's quite the train!

There are two types of stories we can tell ourselves:

1. Stories about *ourselves*
2. Assumptions *about others and the world around us*

In this section, we'll tackle the first. Hot on its heels will be the assumptions we make about the world around us.

When I was trying to unravel the thoughts destroying my happiness, I built a process called the Story Changing Process. The idea is to challenge the stories you're telling yourself and replace them with a new narrative that is much more self-serving and self-appreciating. The outcome of this work will have a significant impact on your ability to be consistent and will eliminate procrastination in any form because it contributes to feelings of positive self-worth.

I used to constantly berate myself, whispering, "*I'm so stupid!*" under my breath. I didn't think I had any good or creative ideas. I didn't think I had what it took to be successful. After I blew up my life, I got in a cycle of renting and would wistfully look at homes in my neighborhood, telling myself I'd never own one again. I'd never go on vacations. I wasn't good enough, smart enough, driven enough.

You will no doubt have your own library of negative narratives. These are the stories we invite to our mental and emotional tables, along with their ringleader, our Dragon. Imagine that all these stories have been yelling you down for years, or even decades. They've been at your table, telling you story after story, and you've believed and acted on them. Until now.

Now you can break that cycle and hit the button that knocks their chairs back, sending them into a vat of boiling oil, just like Dr. Evil did in the Austin Powers movies. It's time to invite new and better stories to your table.

In my first book, *Think Again*, I wrote about this process, and I've since revamped it. It's a simple process, but it's not easy. The trick is to understand the sequence so when a story crops up, you have a quick 1-2-3 way to switch it for something that serves you more fully.

Step 1: Identifying the stories

Write out the stories that tear you down — I'm not good enough, smart enough, too old/young, don't come from the right back-ground, I'll never make it, I'm stupid, and the like. Start with one, get used to the process, and then repeat with the next one. Sometimes people like to make a giant list of stories and then move to Step 2, while others like to do them one at a time. Adapt and evolve this process in whatever way works for you.

Step 2: Refresh the story

In this step, we challenge the old story and replace it with a new one. The new story feeds your GOAT and shows that there are limitless opportunities and solutions. There's no "one way" to do anything, and this new narrative will guide you past the Dragon's barriers and into your greatness.

This step can be tricky. To help you out, I'll give you some examples.

Story: I'm not good enough.
Refresh: I'll figure it out.

Story: I don't deserve good things...
Refresh: If I work hard, I can get anything I want.

Story: I'm stupid.
Refresh: I'm fully capable.

Story: I'm too old.
Refresh: I have so much experience to offer!

Story: I'm not smart enough.
Refresh: "Smart" has nothing to do with it. It's about effort and action. I can control those.

The Refresh Stage is the most powerful because it's bringing new thoughts and ideas to the table. The trick is to have your Refresh stories focus on your ability to control the situation. You control your effort, actions, focus, consistency, attitude, and more.

Step 3: What will you do now?

Action is key to any new process, so the question is what will you do about these new thoughts and ideas? How will you start remembering this simple 1-2-3 process so that when the old stories try to take their seat at your mental dinner table, you boot them out?

Suggestions that may help:

- Write your Refresh story on a sticky note and put it some-where you can see it every day (bathroom, kitchen, desk area, etc.)
- Put a notification on your phone to remind you about the Refresh phrase
- Create a password you enter every day with a new refreshed reminder
- Include the process in your daily meditations

If you don't act on these new thoughts, your belief system will not change. Repetition is the name of the game! Make it a daily part of your life. Kick the old thoughts to the curb and stick 'em on a one-way bus out of your life. Every time you do, your Dragon shrinks a little more. It's got fewer cronies to hang out with. This freaks it out, so expect some of your biggest doubts and fears to start bubbling to the surface. Your Dragon will make it hard to remember the new stories and will bring up all the crappy things it wants you to feel. Look away. Don't invite those stories to stay. See it for what it is: the Dragon is flailing because it's *failing*.

Shrink, Dragon, shrink.

THE ASSUMPTION CHALLENGING PROCESS

Much like we do with stories, we make giant assumptions about the world around us and how people will react to what we say or do. Unlike stories, assumptions are outward facing. We are terrible predictors of other people's behavior, and yet we continually try, making up stories that range from the disconcerting to the downright catastrophic.

Assumptions can be things like:

- People are talking about you behind your back
- Believing no one likes you
- People won't say "yes" to you (so you don't ask for what you want)
- People will mock you (for putting yourself out there)
- It just won't work and you'll look stupid
- You won't get the support you want or need

- Everyone should just *know* what you're thinking and what you want
- What you want to do is so hard that there's no point in starting
- That person is being mean
- No one wants to listen to you
- If you talk to that person, it will blow up and they'll get angry (so you don't do it)
- If you do this thing, it might not make any money (so you don't do it)
- The market/economy/industry will crash

You get the picture. If you are hesitating because you are worried about the way the world or people or your imaginary dragons will respond, then you're making an assumption.

I've been guilty of making massive assumptions that ground my progress to a halt. I avoided doing videos forever because I don't know how to put on makeup, nor do I really know how to style my hair. Thank you, autism, for those gifts! I knew videos would help my business tremendously, but I hesitated for years. Then one day, I figured, *"Hey, people see me like this every day, and no one has run away screaming or stuck a bag over my head. Just do it!"* And so, I did. It has been one of the single biggest reasons for my success, and I inwardly cringe at how many opportunities I missed because I fed into the assumption, instead of my GOAT. Here's the assumptions challenging process. Again, it's a simple 1-2-3. Get out your GOAT-book. You've got more writing to do!

Step 1: What assumptions are you making?

Make a list, just as you did with the stories. Start with one. Start with one hundred. I don't care. That's not the point. The point is what you do with Steps 2 and 3. An assumption is any story you're making up about the future, your industry or market, people, or other subject. It includes predictions you're trying to make and outcomes you're trying to anticipate.

Step 2: Challenge the assumptions

What's really going on? Did people really care about how I looked? NO! Did they throw tomatoes at me when I went on stage? Nope again! The assumptions we make are fictitious stories custom-designed by our Dragon to dissuade us from making advances into unfamiliar areas. Familiar is not good though, so challenging these assumptions and finding them baseless and wrong is key to unlocking more of your GOAT-ness and living the life you want.

Every assumption you make is a tether, nailed to the wall of your comfort zone. It's time to release them.

Here are some examples of Assumptions and their Challengers:

Assumption: People will make fun of me.
Challenge: Their mockery is a function of their own pain and poison, so whatever they have to say is not about me. It's about them.

Assumption: No one wants to listen to me.
Challenge: Someone out there needs what I have to say. Ignore the people for whom it isn't going to appeal and focus on the ones who want it!

Assumption: This isn't going to work.
Challenge: Lots of things don't work, but I'll keep trying different things until one of them does! It's not failure — it's testing.

Assumption: I'm never going to make it.
Challenge: I control how hard I work, and on what. I make my own rules and my own standards. Nothing else matters.

Assumption: I'm going to annoy people when I call or reach out to them.
Challenge: It's only annoying if I let it be that way, so I'll make it worth their time to talk with me. I can control the value I bring to this interaction.

Assumptions are bred from fear, and they multiply as your anxiety grows. The Challenger statements you see above all bring control back to you, so you can do something about the situation. Anxiety cannot exist in the presence of action, so the more you do, the less you fear and the fewer assumptions you make.

Step 3: Living the challenge

Stepping through the assumptions can be harder than stepping through our personal stories because we have to reconcile that we cannot control how anyone is going to react, nor can we predict any future events. The outcomes may be positive, neutral, or negative. What is important is that you see the value you bring and assume that whatever comes your way, you'll deal with it. You'll figure it out. You'll find a way through. You're in control. Your Dragon can only blow fire for so long; it eventually runs out. That's when you know you are winning at challenging your assumptions and your stories. One day, you simply realize how long it has been since those old stories were a part of your life. And you go have ice cream because ice cream is great (on hot days, anyway. I can't eat ice cream in a Canadian winter. It's cold enough!).

ELIMINATING YOUR PAIN IDENTITIES

Sometimes our negative, hurtful stories and assumptions take on a skin. We start identifying personally with the narrative and act accordingly. Most pain identities are rooted in trauma of some kind, no matter how big or small. If you've been told all your life that you're a screw-up and you'll never make it, you start believing this is who you are as a person. You start looking for other ways to act in accordance, and your personality starts to morph and shrink itself into a narrow definition that has been given to you, or you give to yourself (or a combination of both).

Examples of pain identities are things like:

- I'm a perfectionist
- I'm inconsistent
- I have to be perfect
- I'm a screw-up
- I'm an introvert/extrovert
- I don't like people
- I'm only a mid-level producer
- I'm a "high D" on the DISC profile
- I'm an ESTJ on the Myers-Briggs profile
- I'm lazy

- I'm stupid
- I'm nothing
- I'm worthless
- I'm always the victim

We can also have unhealthy identities that perpetuate behaviors that can hold us back or make us very sick:

- I'm a smoker
- I'm unhealthy
- I don't work out
- I don't meditate
- I don't care

In either case, the identity is creating a series of walls, which rise higher and higher as you entrench more in the characteristics of that persona. Pain identities are what appear when fixed mindsets become the only way you think. And fixed mindsets are predicated on "this is who I am and I cannot, will not change." I've worked with people struggling with incredible suffering for absolutely no reason. They're trying to live up to some ideal that is familiar, but it is *not good*. That's how you know that the identity needs to be challenged and converted.

To complicate matters further, you can have more than one identity. I can declare myself to be an introvert (to avoid going to places with people), and I can also call myself unhealthy or lazy. Scores and outcomes on psychological tests like DISC and Myers-Briggs are meant to be a snapshot in time and not a life sentence. These change. You change. And half the time, you're not answering like you currently *are*. You answer the questions much more optimistically than is perhaps true. It's what we do as humans. Admitting that we're not behaving precisely in the best way possible is tough to look at. So, we fudge the numbers to get the outcome we want and then declare it to be "proof" of our inadequacy or station in life.

The good news is there's a way out. You can convert these pain identities into life-serving, soul-fulfilling personas. The process once again is simple, but that doesn't make it easy. The process is similar to the Story Changing and Assumption Challenging processes, but with a twist at the end.

Get out your GOAT-book. Here's how it works:

Step 1: Identify the identity

Clearly identify the persona or identity you've created for your-self. Awareness is always the first step. It's not easy to admit that we've boxed ourselves in, creating protective layers around how we view ourselves. But once you do, you can move on to the following steps to start converting it to something that feeds your heart, mind, and spirit. A pain identity is something that, when you finally acknowledge it, makes you cringe a little. It may also conjure memories of oppression by individuals, organizations, relationships, situations, and more. This part is not fun, but it's 100% necessary.

Step 2: Where did it come from?

Did you give this definition to yourself, or has it been handed to you by others, whether consciously or not? Where did the identity originate, and who perpetuated it? This could be parents, teachers, mentors, companies where we work, industry standards we feel we have to live up to, and so on.

Step 3: Developing new identities

In this stage, you convert the negative, hurtful identity into some-thing new. It should play to your strengths and open more doors to opportunity and advancement in the direction you want you to go in life.

Old: Perfectionist
New: Fully capable

Old: Introvert
New: Selectively social

Old: I'm a screw-up.
New: I can take control of my life and refuse to be judged by others.

Old: I'm lazy.

New: I probably just need to give myself some instructions on what to do. I just don't know how.

Old: I'm a high "C" on the DISC profile.

New: I'm a C today. Wonder what I'll be next week?

Old: I'm terrible at writing.

New: I'm untrained at writing. I can learn and improve!

The new way of talking with yourself is once again bringing control back to you, and beginning to give you faith in your abilities to create a truly great life. With every identity you shift into the positive side, the easier this becomes, because as the walls begin to crumble, you start to get a taste of the beauty of what's on the other side. And that is more refreshing than rain on a hot day.

Step 4: Planning ahead for triggers

If you've held this old identity for a long time, it will be harder to convert, simply because you've spent a long time building these neural pathways in your brain. Knowing what situations may trip you up or threaten to push you back into the old way of being is key to never letting the Dragon win another round.

Think of the old identity you want to rid yourself of. Are there situations that might trigger an outburst, or that may make you shrink back into the shadows? What can you do differently — or should you avoid certain situations or people altogether? You always have a choice. You may need to make a different one now than you did before.

Step 5: The trigger phrase

This final step is one you can repeat to yourself when old habits and stories rear their ugly heads. When your Dragon whispers the same old horrible story in your ear, what will you say to yourself to prevent it from convincing you to revert to your old ways? A trigger phrase is the equivalent of Dorothy, *in the Wizard of Oz*, repeating over and over, "Lions and Tigers and Bears, oh my!" as she skipped down the golden path, arm in arm with the Tin Man and the Lion. She was going to save Oz, and nothing would stop her. She was going to be brave.

Some phrases I've used to help me take those big steps are:

- I've got this
- I'll figure it out
- The new me is (insert word or phrase)
- Goodbye Dragon, not today
- Everything is going to be okay
- What am I going to do about it?

Pain is a part of life, but it's not supposed to be self-inflicted. If you put your beautiful bird, with the song that is your own, in a box, it will eventually stop singing. Don't lose your voice. Don't lose your glow. The Dragon within you shrinks yet again when you challenge the pain it's trying to give you. Don't take that flaming bag of poop. Give it back and turn your attention to an identity that fulfills and brings joy to your life.

Just because you have pain doesn't mean you deserve it.

FROM FILTH TO FERTILIZER

The From Filth to Fertilizer process is one of my favorites, not because it has swear words in it (though that is a plus), but because it's a methodology by which I removed all the pain and hurt from my past and turned it into something useful. Trauma, big and small, sucks. It hurts. Our Dragon files these memories away somewhere easily accessible so we can bring them up any time something similar happens, scaring ourselves back into "safety."

Life can be tough. Really tough. And thanks to how the brain is designed, we remember all the most traumatic parts. We can feel the same pain today as we did when the crappy situation happened. You break up with your boyfriend, who drove a blue car. Now every time you see a blue car, you burst into tears. You got fired from your last job, so now every time someone says, "Want to have a chat?" you run to the bathroom and hope they forget about you. I had so many triggers from the church that even long after I'd left, every day felt like I was reliving my past. I was shamed and made to feel horrifically guilty. I took it so personally that if I saw someone from the church at the mall, I'd instantly feel like I'd done something wrong. Surely I was wearing my hair wrong or was shopping at the wrong place. If I was wearing pants instead of a skirt, I'd legit run and hide (pants were a huge no-no). To this day, seeing people that even *look* like the people from that church makes my heart skip. But at least it's only a skip and not a full-on panic attack.

We should not live in fear of the past re-triggering us or being recreated in our present lives. I realized that I had to do something when I'd react incredibly emotionally to something Marc said that most definitely didn't warrant such a strong response. The past came roaring back into my heart, my mind went blank, and I just exploded, the pain was so great. It scared me.

The only way to prevent something from re-triggering you is to take out its fuse. Clearly my fuse was really, really short. I had to remove the pain and replace it with something else so that when I met with the same situation again, I'd just let it go by. Considering how volcanic I became, that seemed impossible until I mapped out a way to identify the root of the reaction — and then took away its power. This is the crux of the "From Filth to Fertilizer" process: remove the power your past has over you, and your present becomes an oasis of calm.

Here's how it works:

Step 1: Identify the situation

The first step in everything is awareness and acceptance. It happened. It sucked. But to simply "move on" or "forget about it" is impossible. You can never "let it go" because it's a part of you. You can't outrun your past. But you can change what happens to you when it comes sliding back into your life. So give it a name, this difficult time in your life. And let's start dealing with it.

Step 2: Define and accept how you feel about it

Yup! Those beautiful, magical emotions are back again! Using the Emotion Wheel, write down all of the words that pop up — good and bad. Contradictions are okay. Just be open and accepting of what stands out to you.

Step 3: Converting From Filth to Fertilizer

This step is where you take the fangs out of your trauma or pain. When someone tried on two occasions to kill my fledgling business, I was crushed. *"Why would they do that? I thought they loved me."* I sat with that pain for years until I put it to the test with this process. When I really looked at what was going on, the person who had tried to kill my business *did* love me, but their fear about what I was doing was so great that they didn't want me to suffer (they'd suffered a huge business-related loss and it took their soul away. They have never been the same since). I found this explanation useful and was able to keep that close relationship, knowing that it was their fear that drove their actions, and it was, for them, more powerful than their love. It was hard to swallow, but it made sense. I pity them now but was able to repair the relationship and find their love acceptable again.

The hardest step is finding the good and the useful in the pain. Ask yourself what you can take from a crappy situation that can be converted into an excellent lesson for you or those around you. I learned to have compassion for those who judged and rejected me. They weren't doing it to me; they were doing it to themselves. They were so full of hate and resentment, and I was such an easy target. Now I feel sorry for them. They're small, weak, and in pain. I can't change them, and I definitely don't like them, but I can see them in a different, pain-free light. It wasn't about me, and that phrase has kept me from going nuclear on many another person who's come at me with their viciousness and anger since. Finding a lesson in our pain can be a wonderful rehabilitation process. You are not alone in your pain, but you also don't have to dwell in it either. Your pain is not your home; your home is wherever you decide to build your castle. As you tear down the walls of shame and guilt and switch your perspective on past situations, no matter how horrible, your castle becomes stronger, and your world becomes brighter and full of opportunities.

You cannot see light and goodness in people if you anticipate that everyone is out to get you. The more you stay in your painful past, the more convinced you become that everyone will do the same to you forever. The From Filth to Fertilizer process guides you away from the terrors and the tears, and gives you the ability to move past anything or anyone that stands in your way.

It's not about being perfect — it's about progress.

HAPPINESS TRIGGERS

One thing your Dragon cannot stand is when you're happy. The good news is, we're going to really irritate the Dragon by generating happiness in five different ways. Happiness is underrated. If you're happy and you know it, you don't just clap your hands. You do the hard work. You make routines work for you. You surround yourself with people who contribute to your joy instead of those who suck you emotionally dry.

Happy people are successful people, not because they're millionaires or billionaires (most of those people are miserable anyway). They may have modest houses and decent but not flashy cars. They're successful for the simple reason that they have the exact life they want. I don't need to make a million dollars to be happy. I've made a million dollars. I didn't like it. It's not that making millions is a bad thing. It just can't be the *point*.

I was first introduced to "happiness triggers" in Brendon's *High Performance Habits* book and have since taught a series of workshops to broadcast these strategies. They remind us of the good within ourselves, others, and the world that we live in. I encourage you to think of additional ways to generate the joy you want. A life full of joy that no one can ever take away is a life worth living. Do not blame the world if you are unhappy. Do something about it! I always knew happiness is a choice but didn't know what choices to make! Exactly *how* do you "choose" happiness? Well, I've got five ways you can choose happiness, and it's just to get you started.

Doorframe trigger

A doorframe trigger is simply a phrase or image that you put on a doorframe you enter and exit frequently. It might be your office door, the front door, the bathroom door — it doesn't matter. To initiate this trigger, every time you walk through that door, you remind yourself of something or someone to appreciate. You already know how valuable appreciation truly is. Now you have a way to remind yourself to show that appreciation many times a day!

I have a happy face on my doorframe. I typically only leave my office to make a tea, have lunch, or go to the bathroom. I send a quick text or make a quick call and tell the person what they mean to me, or how their work has helped or inspired me that day. Or I just call to say hi, and that I was thinking about them. When you train your brain to appreciate others, it creates powerful neural pathways, shrinks the Dragon, and lifts the spirits. With repetition, you get the results faster. If more success, higher income, stronger relationships, or more self-love is what you want, happiness is your gateway, and repetitive triggers like this one help you form that path deeply and quickly.

Alarm trigger

In Brendon's book, he calls these "notification" triggers, but I like alarms better. Notifications are easy to ignore or get mixed in with a bunch of other things. Alarms require you to physically turn them off.

Heidi, one of my clients, did these in the most hilarious and effective way. She wanted to remember to be intentional with her time. So, at 9:00 am, her phone's alarm went off and the notification said, "Be Intentional!" Since she wanted anyone working with her to *also* be intentional, she'd shout from her office, "Be intentional!" In the open-concept office in which she works, you can imagine what happened. Now, at 9:00 am, *everyone* in the office shouts back, "Be intentional!" and then they all get to work.

If you trigger these alarms in your day to remind you to be happy, tell yourself one of your refresh stories, or just scan the world for something that brings you joy, it's like Pavlov's dog: any time an alarm goes off, you'll think happy, lovely thoughts.

Waiting trigger

I don't know about you, but I love waiting in line and looking around. Starbucks in the morning is my favorite because the one by me is full of baristas chatting and laughing together. I love to see people laugh. It's hard *not* to laugh when others are giggling around you. There have been social experiments about this, and it's true! The waiting trigger is designed to have you look around wherever and whenever you're waiting and find something in the area to appreciate. This trains your brain to see the world as good and to be thankful for something, no matter how small. When you believe the world to be a safe and good place, it can alleviate anxiety and worry in a big way. Plus, the double-whammy impact of also feeling appreciation, whether you say something or not, is a strong Dragon-shrinker.

Gift trigger

Gift triggers are a way to know if the work you've been doing on your self-worth has succeeded or is still in progress. The "gift trigger" is a compliment or a physical thing that someone gives you and how you learn to accept it.

I told you about the workshop where people were grouped in twos and had to compliment each other, and all the recipient had to say was, "thank you." Oh, the cringing! The deflection! It was both funny and painful to watch. They realized that they viewed themselves far less favorably than how they were perceived by others.

When you receive a gift, whether verbal or physical, the idea here is to hold onto that gift, see the value shown to you by the giver, and feel the warmth of that emotion. Someone is showing you gratitude. To reject or deflect it is to insult them. It doesn't matter if you were just "doing your job"; they saw extra value and wanted to express it to you.

To say "thanks" and truly mean it, without even a flicker of "I don't really deserve this," means you've made massive progress on the emotional front.

Stress triggers

These aren't triggers that create stress; they're trigger phrases that help you get out of a stressful situation. I have a horrible habit of worrying incessantly about my children, my work, and my future. Life is hard. People let us down. University is lonely for my son, and I can worry nonstop about him making friends and having a good experience as he grows into adulthood.

I love to push myself, try new things, and set deadlines. But sometimes this works against me if things don't go according to plan, and I can set myself into a pattern of fretting, fussing, and sweating it out at 2:00 am. Now, however, I see the stress rising up, and instead of succumbing to it, I ask myself: "*What can I do about it?*" I picked this phrase very intentionally. For me to remove my anxiety or stress, I have to take back the controls from the Dragon. My Dragon loves to torment me, but it has no power when I'm in charge. Moving toward a solution negates anxiety because I'm no longer worrying, I'm doing.

Your phrase can be anything from "It's going to be okay" to "I've got this" to "I'll figure it out." Create a phrase for yourself now, and get ready to arm yourself with it the next time your Dragon strikes.

Password triggers

This was an idea someone presented to me recently at a conference. He wanted to remind himself every day about a certain phrase that encourages him to keep moving toward his goals. To do that, he created a password with his happiness phrase in it. Every day, he'd type those words, reaffirm them in his head, and keep going. It's like the doorframe trigger for your computer!

Happiness is self-generated. The world around you can help, but you cannot depend on it to uplift you and keep you going. You are the source of happiness, and if you need more of it in your life, do not ask the world to step in. That's up to you, and thankfully, accessing your joy is easier than you think.

THE DANGER OF "WHY"

Your Dragon's favorite way to start a question is with "*Why?*" I intentionally avoid asking "why" type questions because they do nothing but make my audience feel defensive and in trouble. It backs people into a corner and makes them argumentative. You learned this language from your Dragon. It will torture you with questions like, "*Why aren't you where you should be? Why is it so hard to do this, when it's really just an easy thing? Why am I like this? Why can't I just be better? Why? Why? Why?*"

It's a nasty road that does nothing but feed into catastrophic thinking, low self-esteem, and a destroyed soul. So, change the question. Instead of "why" change it to "what, how, where," or "when." You can use this strategy with your internal monologue, or with anyone in your life — kids, spouses, team members, employees, and anyone that you care about. Creating open conversations that end well can lead to a much more peaceful existence for everyone.

Here are some examples:

Dragon: Why didn't you do your work last week?
GOAT: What was it about last week that made doing the work so hard?

Dragon: Why am I so bad at this?
GOAT: How can I learn to be better at this?

Dragon: Why can't you think for yourself?
GOAT: What is it that you find so difficult about making up your own mind?

When you remove the defensiveness of "why" questions, you become an explorer. This is especially important if you have kids, a team, or work with anyone you're trying to guide through life or business. You don't *mean* to shut them down with inadvertent "why" questions, but you do.

The next time you have to ask someone about something they've done, or not done, switch the script: start with "what" or literally anything other than "why," and you'll find that you both feel better about the conversation and get to the solution faster!

DON'T BE A "HERO"

Sometimes, we want to be heroes. If you've had a tough go in life and learned some hard lessons, you often turn around and try to "save" people in similar situations. You want to make it easier for them. You give them everything they need. You hand them ready-to-go programs and processes. You literally spell out for them what they need to do. And yet they don't do it. They often become resentful of your help. *WT actual F?*

Your Dragon really loves the hero in you. It constantly wants to feel needed, valued, and relevant. The hero loves to have all the answers and feels absolutely amazing when yet another acolyte wanders from a conversation, having been blessed by their knowledge. The hero could let them figure it out, but it's faster if he just tells them. They should be happy — he just literally gave them the answer! Their lives should be so simple! But time and time again, the hero is disappointed. Nothing happens. I've had countless conversations with leaders who scratch their heads, wondering why week after week their teams stagnate, don't show up to meetings, and wander around like lost puppies.

The solution to cure you of the hero complex is simple. Instead of giving people the answer, simply ask them, *"What do you think you should do about it?"*

Nine times out of ten, they already know it anyway; they're just too chicken to bring it up first. They don't want to look stupid in case they're wrong. I have a client whose entire office has been trained to "ask permission" from the boss before they do anything. No one has ever gotten in trouble, and the guy at the top even recognizes he's been acting like a hero. But nothing will change unless the hero stops giving answers, solutions, and strategies, demanding instead that people come up with their own ideas. This one particular leader hasn't, and he gets more and more angry with his team. They're not producing, and he's losing money. Instead of challenging them to come up with their own solutions, he tries to give them even *more* ideas, clouding an already-full roster of strategies they're not using.

Shoot your Dragon in the foot a few times and stop being the hero. Challenge people to think for themselves. Don't give in to the temptation to give them the answer (it will be hard, so staple your lips shut if you have to!). As people discover that they've had the answers all along, their confidence grows by leaps and bounds. You'll build a way stronger team, corporate environment, or family.

THE LANGUAGE OF COMMITMENT

Your Dragon is an expert at deluding you into believing you're committing to something. It might be doing it right now! You may have read the strategies above, and said, "*I should do those things!*" and feel all awesome and self-satisfied. You *said* you'd do it, right? Not so fast!

Language is important. Words matter. And the words you use to establish whether or not you're actually going to do something are critical.

Think of something you want to commit to: implementing a strategy from this book, eating better, going to the gym, making calls, and so on. Now think of a phrase you can say to yourself that shows "commitment."

It might sound like these (I will use "eating better" as the example):

- I'm going to try to eat better.
- I wish I could eat better.
- I want to eat better!
- I've got to start eating better. I have to start eating better!
- I hope I can start eating better I should start eating better.

Did you know that if you've used any of these phrases, you actually *did not commit* to eating better? These are your Dragon's spin doctors going to work. It sounds like you're committed, but your brain doesn't light up at all. There were no instructions to act differently *now*, because all of those phrases put the actual event into the future. So for now, the brain registers nothing and goes on its merry little way.

There's really only *one* way to talk to yourself about commitment, and it sounds like this:

"I'm eating better right now, starting with breakfast."

There are two things here: the first is using present-type language. When you speak to yourself in present language, you tell your brain, "*Hey, brain! Start your engines and get moving! Find me some opportunities to make this happen!*" Your brain will then kick into high gear, find all the ways for you to eat better, and give you the motivation to act accordingly.

The second is giving yourself a deadline or a target. In this example, it was "breakfast." It's a specific time in the day when this new habit is going to be put to the test. Commitments are always about things that are important to you, whether it's dinner with your spouse, personal care, doing necessary and results-generating work, or creating time to think and meditate so your brain can rest. For as many times as you stopped doing something, you eventually started up again. Success is in getting up, brushing yourself off, and taking another step, however shaky. And the better you get at speaking high-commitment language, the more likely you are to never fall off the wagon again!

IMPROVE SLEEP

Sleep. Your Dragon loves to keep you from it. It keeps you up so you can't go to sleep. Mine likes to wake me up at 2:00 am so I can fret about something. Maybe yours shakes you awake with anxious thoughts around 4:00 am and then prevents you from getting back to dreamland.

Dragons are sneaky sleep-deprivers, and this can have serious health side effects. If you want to scare yourself, just Google it. High blood pressure, diabetes, heart attack or heart failure, obesity, and poor brain function. Terrifying stuff ! Sleep is necessary to create long-term memories, for weight loss, for stress relief, and hundreds of other things. And yet we can fall into horrific sleep patterns, wreaking havoc on our lives.

I love Bill O'Hanlon's solutions to sleep problems in *Do One Thing Different*. If you can't go to sleep, or wake up and toss and turn, after fifteen minutes get up and do something you *hate*. I hate mental math and push-ups. When I woke up worrying about my kids at 2:00 am, unable to fall back to sleep, I started going through multiplication tables. My brain hated that so much, I drifted off to sleep. If multiplication didn't work, I'd have had to do push-ups, and I hate those more than math. When your brain doesn't want to do something, it gets very, very tired. So don't get up and read, play video games, or do something you actually like. Fold the laundry. Do push-ups. Stain the floor. Stand on your head.

A really interesting thing happens when you train your brain to believe that waking up when you want to sleep is bad: it stops waking up. It's like, *"No thank you! That doesn't look fun."* You trick your Dragon at its own game! It always avoids the hard thing, so give it a hard thing to do when you want to sleep, and ta-da, slumber time!

WHAT WILL YOU DO NOW?

You cannot slay your Dragon because it controls important life-giving functions, but you can shrink it to the point where it doesn't have power over you. Through targeted strategies, you can shrink its size, take away its ability to cause pain and suffering, remove its fangs, and make room for your amazing and talented GOAT self. Remove your Dragon and its cronies from your emotional table, and replace them with better guests. You'll find your life falling in line with what you really want.

My clients never start working on growth strategies for their businesses, at least not at first. To begin, I focus on removing obstacles from their path — obstacles they put there themselves but just didn't have the tools to remove. They didn't even see them. But when you choose to remove these obstacles — those stories, assumptions, behaviors, and identities that keep you stuck in a cold, dark box — your greatness starts to take root and every aspect of your life changes for the better. Your box may be so dark you think you're blind. Reach up, remove the blindfolds, and walk through the box. It's only made of paper.

With these strategies, you will shrink your Dragon and step into your GOAT life.

BOOK 3

STEPPING INTO YOUR GOAT LIFE

Despite finding out relatively recently that I'm autistic, leading me to complete acceptance of who I am, I have been working toward living my GOAT life for a while. Running my agency seemed to be one massive headache after another. It wasn't even profitable. I was bolstering the bottom line with coaching and speaking gigs. I knew it wasn't a good business model, nor one that would sustain me. It was killing me to work ninety hours a week, taking on the constant pressure of getting approvals (or rejections) for work I'd done.

When I decided to move into performance coaching and started to really dig into that work, it felt like home. I can see now that I'd been building my "home" — that place of safety, fulfillment, meaning, and joy — in other things and other people. I pegged my value on whether I had X or Y number of clients, or made a million dollars a year. And when my clients dwindled and the money started to run out, particularly when the pandemic hit, I had no choice: I had to start building my home within.

I decided I was sick of being unhappy. Life was too short. And while I had a pretty good idea of what made me happy, I hadn't nailed it down to specifics — the business model that suited me best, the ideal team/partnership structure, the work, and so on. I tried and tested a whack of things, not all of which worked. Most didn't, in fact. I can create online courses with ease, but no one logs onto them. While I can make lots of money, I'm not here for the money: I'm here for the results. So, I stopped doing them.

I conducted group coaching for a long time, but most people invested a smaller amount (versus my private client fees) because they didn't believe in themselves. This translates, in large part, to people not showing up, not doing the work, or just complaining. That's not my cup of tea either. So, I stopped and have replaced it with a new coaching program for those who can't afford my big-ass fees. It's harder to get in than the former group coaching program, but those restrictions make people put in more effort. They show up, do the work, and get the results. The work I do lines up with what drives my joy and fulfillment.

When my super-elites started to talk about how they wish they could meet other super-elites, I created an exclusive Mastermind, called Tribe of GOATs. The relationships fostered there have been nothing short of magical, and the results breathtaking.

I work precisely how much I wish. I make exactly what I want to make to live life to the fullest. I take on only the clients I truly love, who are ready for action. And I leave it all behind when I'm ready to go hang out with my most amazing husband, my friends, and whatever kids are home at the time (three are currently in college/university, one is home, still making his way through high school).

I don't worry about where the money will come from because I have learned to trust that I will figure it out. I don't wake up fretting and sweating at 2:00 am, terrified something will go wrong, because I am 100% in control of my world. I don't feel bad about not having partners or a team; it doesn't make me feel unsuccessful. It makes me feel empowered to make my own choices. I work from home because people make me tired. The point is that I work, live, and love based on how I want to do these things, not how the world thinks I should.

I'm building and improving my life daily, consciously and intentionally. There are times when I didn't think I had the strength to take it all on. When I decided to close my agency, initially I let clients go through attrition. The pandemic sped that up considerably, and I wasn't ready (who was?). My income went to zero, and Marc carried the household. When we married, I promised him I'd contribute half of all our expenses, so not living up to that felt like betrayal.

My Dragon hollered constantly that I was going to flirt with bankruptcy for the third time. It brought up my shame, fear, and imposter syndrome. I was going to coach people to be high performers — who did I think I was? I'd never done it before. I'd taught marketing and social media for ten years. I did the work for people. Coaching was getting my *clients* to do the work, so would they? Could I get them off their asses to make big, scary changes? This was different. Who would care?

It's important to know that as you go through the process of defining and living your true GOAT life, your Dragon will get really, really mad. It will throw everything it has at you, desperate to keep its pride of place at the head of your table, with all its cronies hooting and hollering with it. It will bring up your past, throw it in your face, and try to scare you with it. You may get sick. You may have an accident. Something around you might stop working — something you've depended upon for a long time. People may start acting funny, either pulling away or drawing closer than before.

You'll hit your "upper limit." I've experienced it many times, and you will too. Whenever I hit the edge of my comfort zone, I feel like my world is vibrating and could collapse at any time. I'm afraid, but I've taught myself that fear is good, and it can't hold me back. I hold on, keep going; soon enough the Dragon goes quiet. My goal is to have your Dragon lose fight after fight after fight, so your GOAT has a chance to make its way to the light of day. You have everything you need to make this a reality. All the answers, ideas, motivation, confidence, and energy. You just need to find them, dust them off, and use them.

When her world collapsed everywhere around her, Mel thought she was down for the count. It was heartbreaking to hear her voice, usually so confident, sound so frail and confused. We went through the Emotion Wheel together that day and she realized something: she felt *good* about things, in addition to feeling absolutely devastated. There was resilience within her that would carry her forward. In the volcanic events of her life back then, for a time, everyone and everything she used to lean on for support vanished. She had nowhere to hide and no one to whom she could hand her problems. Gone. While I was sad that her support network had blown up, I was also glad: she'd finally meet the super awesome, strong, competent, and amazing human I knew was in there all along. Sometimes, things have to go sideways in a big way for us see our true spirit, resilience and ability to stand up under our own power.

You have what it takes to live a GOAT life right now. You don't deserve it; you earn it. It won't come to you; you have to move toward it. And as you do, while constructing carefully around you the things that deliver boundless joy, fulfillment, income, and success, you'll start to really love it. Then one day, you'll look around and see nothing but the things you love the most, and it will feel amazing.

I'd like to invite you on the journey to your GOAT-ness. What follows are a series of strategies to define your GOAT-ness more clearly so you can start constructing the life that suits you best. You will try things, and they won't work. GOATs know this. Just start something else. You'll get there. Remember that your Dragon is never gone, so don't give it the time of day. Keep going because you won't want to miss what lies ahead.

HOW TO FEED YOUR GOAT

We're going to explore a series of GOAT-feeding strategies, some of which will appeal to you and some will not. What matters is that you look at each one critically and ask yourself if you are already a GOAT in that department. I firmly believe in our ability to always improve, so I never count myself out of any options. I practice my GOAT habits and mindsets continuously, every day, even though it may look like I've mastered them. I have not, and that's incredibly exciting because if I can make myself even happier than I am now, I'm all for it!

As with the Dragon-Shrinking strategies, evolve and adapt your GOAT habits with your brain's wiring, your direction in life, your emotional state, and your passions. These are starting points. Like when you go to yoga class (and I say "you" because I don't go — classes of any kind are not my thing), if you have injuries, they allow you to modify the exercises. This will be no different. Modify, adapt, evolve, and add to (but don't take away from) each of these.

I also recommend you choose one to start with, and then once you've got it down to a science, move on to the next one. There's no value in trying to bite off a big chunk. Small steps lead to the biggest changes, and patience is required. Considering how badly I suck at patience, if I can do this, you can too.

I'm ready to bring out your GOAT if you are! Let's DO this!

WHAT MAKES YOU HAPPY?

To move into your GOAT life, the best place to start is to identify what makes you happy. Few people take the time to ask, let alone answer the question, but it's the most critical part of your path to GOAT-ness. Happy people do the hard work. They are successful. They sleep well and take care of themselves. They're never out of control. Happiness is pervasive once you adopt it as your primary goal in life. You've already got happiness triggers, but we're taking this a step or two further.

Nathalie, one of my private clients, constructed a life where she could travel nearly five to six months of the year but still sell enough real estate to fund her life *and* increase her savings. The sun literally *shone* from her entire body. She was doing what most people only dream of. The last time we talked, she'd just booked a Club Med stay in Marrakech, Morocco. Then she was going to Scotland. She was living a fabulous life entirely of her choosing. Steven's eyeballs disappear into his smiling face regularly because he's getting closer and closer to his ideal GOAT life. I think "running my business from the Bahamas" is still where we're headed, and it's going to be a really fun ride getting there. For others, happiness is being precisely where they are and feeling truly content with what they're doing. The very definition of "happiness" is so personal and so unique. No one can explain what makes you happy — only you can. It's okay for something to make you happy when it doesn't even register for someone else. Who cares? You're not living their life — you're living *yours*. Your GOAT journey is deeply personal. I don't care what anyone else is doing. We are influenced by the rich and famous, and can assume that that's the life we want. But when you watch documentaries, you often find that those same people whom you may aspire to be like wish they were anyone but themselves.

Success does not guarantee happiness.

To answer the question *"what makes you happy?"* I will break it down into categories. These are in no particular order, so do the work as you like. Get out that GOAT-book again. This is some of the most important work you can do.

One last piece of advice: don't get stuck in *"how do I make this happen?"* This exercise is first to determine what you *want*. Until you have that, logistics don't matter and can be more of a distraction and dream-killer. So stick with what you want. Trust that you'll figure out *how* later. Your brain will help you, but you have to point it in the right direction first.

Step 1: What work makes you happy?

If you could do something in your business or career all day and every day that wouldn't really feel like "work," what would that be? I love doing deep work with people, so one-on-one coaching and exclusive, small-group masterminds are my jam. I have nearly double the client load of what most coaches in my industry take on, but I'm happy to do it. It's fun; I have the time, and the results are incredible. It's not work. It's easy.

What work do you love most? Is it team-based work, or lone-wolf stuff? I have clients who love coaching because it's all about being a part of the client's progress. Other people absolutely hate it and prefer consulting because they like to hand over the answers, help with the implementation, and then it's "see ya!" A semi-retired client takes people to lunch to prospect instead of making calls. My broker client loves to teach and offers courses and programs for prospects to join. They call him so he doesn't have to make outbound calls. He hates making calls.

I hate making calls too, so I do workshops and presentations at conferences and events. This is sufficient to fill my coaching and mastermind programs. It's brilliant and I love it.

It's your turn now. What WORK makes you happiest? Write down everything that applies.

Step 2: What level of income would make you happy?

I never suggest setting money goals as the only thing to strive for. But let's be honest: to get what you want, you need to be able to afford it. In your quest for true happiness, you have to know how much money you really want to make in order to live the life you want.

When you set an income goal, even a loose one, it allows you to start planning and visualizing what your future life will be like and to get really excited about it.

This can be a "quick and dirty," back of the envelope kind of number, or you can go into elaborate mathematical equations and formulas on a spreadsheet. It doesn't matter. What matters is what level of income do you want to fund the awesome things you want to do?

When you match your income goal with the work that makes you happy, how to achieve it becomes simple. Since happy people do the hard work, pressing beyond fear, motivated by the life they want to lead, it's no wonder they exceed the goals they set.

For some, income is not the point. It's not the point for me, not entirely. I grew up wealthy, but saw what it does to people. But there are things we want to do, places we want to go, and people we want to help, and money gives us the power to do all of that, and more. It's not how much money you make; it's what you *do with it* that matters.

Write that number down. We'll deal with it in a bit!

Step 3: What schedule makes you happy?

I love to make up my own schedule. Until I took on a few extra clients, I kept Mondays and Fridays open. Now my days are fuller, but I still have lots of wiggle room for other work. I don't want to work evenings or weekends. I like a little flexibility to do other things if I so choose, and to go on vacation without having to worry about how my business is faring while I'm away. I like breaks in my day because I get tired and may need a ten-minute nap. Or longer. Whatever. I like time for lunch because that's when I refresh myself and get ready for what the afternoon will bring.

I work out in the morning and never start work before 9:00 am. I prefer 9:30 or 10:00 am. I like to be done by five, but I make some concessions for my West Coast clients who are three hours behind me. While I may be making adjustments and letting things slide a bit, I'm *choosing* to do it. I'm fully in control of my schedule every day.

If you could map out your ideal schedule, which can include your morning or evening routines, plus the way you manage your time at work, what would it look like? Be specific, and you can also be flexible. Every day can be totally different. It's your GOAT life. You write the rules!

Step 4: What environment do you like?

I love to work from home. Office politics scare the life out of me, mostly because I suck at reading people, and diplomacy is not my strong suit. I tend to say what I mean, and sometimes it's not exactly the most polished delivery. I'd been working from home long before the pandemic made it a thing, and I love it. I can be productive, energized, and motivated all day long. Nothing distracts me because I've trained myself to put all the non-work stuff to either before 9:00 am, after 5:00 pm, or the weekend.

Do you love working around people, alone, or a mixture? Heidi, another one of my private clients, became a productivity maven when she moved back to the office after things opened up. Having suffered the tremendous and unexpected loss of her husband, getting back on her feet during the pandemic seemed impossible. Every strategy we used just didn't really click.

But then she went back to the office every day, and now I can barely keep up with her! She has launched a new workshop on planning your life so the unexpected doesn't catch you in the same way it did for her. She's moving and shaking with it, plus doing a thousand other things in her real estate business, some of which she'd neglected for nearly three years. The environment change was everything for her.

What is the ideal environment for you? Define it specifically – alone, office, mix of the two, working from a café … they all qualify, as long as they bring you joy.

Step 5: What people make you happy?

Ah, people. I have such a love/hate relationship with them! On one hand they fascinate me, and on the other they tire me right out. This "people" question can be taken a number of ways, and I invite you to figure out which way you want to define this for yourself.

a)   People you hang around

You will become the average of the people around you. Some people think others won't affect them, that they can somehow avoid their influence. But it's part of our DNA and how we are wired, so there's no escaping it.

Are your friends, office colleagues, and anyone else in your life as excited as you are about making progress, or are they holding on to old habits and ideals? Are they happy people to be around or dragging you down with complaints? Take stock: who's there? Who needs to go? Is there someone who maybe you can spend less/more time with?

b)   Clients

I work with a specific type of client and rarely deviate. I'm picky because the wrong client doesn't get results. It doesn't make sense to get someone to pay for my time just to end up frustrated or overwhelmed. Who is your ideal client? Define them specifically – industry, number of years in their career or business, personal traits if they apply, ambition, and so on. The more you tell your brain what to look for in a perfect client, the greater chance you'll have in finding them!

c)   Office people

If you work in an office, what type of people do you want to be around *in* that office? Are they open and sharing? Are you all like a family? Driven and competitive? Do you love leaderboards? Do you love public recognition? What do you need from the people around you to feel like that place is "home"? Do you spend time chatting with them, or do you prefer to be left alone? How much do you collaborate and strategize with these people, and how do they make you better?

The people in your world contribute significantly to your ability to live a GOAT life. This step cannot be discounted. The more you define the types of people you want in your life, the easier a time you'll have building the life you want. If you want to build a house, you don't draw a sketch on the back of an envelope. You get a detailed, multi-page, CAD-drawn masterpiece, and then you simply follow the instructions on how to build it.

This is the same process we're embarking upon here. Define, refine, execute — live the GOAT life!

Why defining happiness is a "must"

Darren Hardy wrote forty pages of notes on the woman he wanted. Then he wrote another forty on how he needed to show up differently in the world to attract this beautiful creature. If he was going to be happy, he had to tell his brain what to look for, both within and without. The more detailed his description, the clearer the instructions on what he wanted his mind to see in the world. That way, as soon as the right woman waltzed into his life, he'd be ready — and he was.

This is what you're doing here. Be descriptive. Go bananas. Happiness is something you can have in every area of your life, in every way. It's a choice you make every day — to live your happiest life, no matter what's going on. Decide on what will make you happy, from your work, income, people, environment, and anything else you can think of. As you have already learned, GOATs don't force things. They know what they want and will not compromise until they get it.

LIVING LIFE ON YOUR TERMS

Unbeknownst to us, our default state is to strive to live up to everyone else's standards, imitate their lives, run someone else's business, and have someone else's relationships. When I write it like that, it sounds ridiculous; yet that's precisely what most of us do — and it's certainly what I did for most of my life.

We are taught two conflicting truths as children: On one side, we're taught to dream, and that we can do anything. But on the other, we're told to conform to the school system, get a job, get married, have kids, join the PTA, work our tail off, travel a little, then retire and die. At work, we have to conform to the structure of the organization, its levels of achievement, and how they define us. We have to stand out, but not too much; compete, but not too aggressively. It's no wonder the world is full of burnouts. How can we possibly keep up with these moving targets and unrealistic expectations?

The answer is simple: get rid of those outdated rules and write your own. When you live up to your own expectations, they don't move, get switched, change, or disappear unless you make it happen. The world becomes more predictable. Cleaner, safer, and more secure. You're in control, and GOATs know that being in control is *the* answer to a successful and peaceful life.

If you're working for an organization, you may say, *"I don't have control. I'm told what to do and if I don't, I get fired."* This is true.

So don't work somewhere harboring expectations that don't match your own. That you *can* control. You may or may not be some-where that suits you right now, so take stock of your situation, and as we move through the process of setting your expectations and writing your own rule book, cast an eye around. Does it live up to your expectations? Is change in your future? Be patient. Plan properly, and your next move will be fantastic.

We've already covered the power of identifying what makes you happy. Now it's time to set your own standards of excellence and define what "success" looks like.

There are two major steps in this process:

1. Clarifying your GOAT Self
2. Your personal best cheat sheet

Let's start with clarifying your GOAT self. Just like finding the right life partner, you need to give your brain instructions on how you want to show up in the world. We will be training your brain to look for every opportunity to step up into your GOAT self, but first we have to define what that even *is*.

Typically, you will have a few "GOAT selves" because you will act ever so slightly differently based on the situation. I have a "GOAT self " as a mother, a wife, a business owner, and a friend. If you coach kids, there's another GOAT self you need to define. Belong to the community in some way? That's another opportunity.

Defining your "GOAT self " does two things: First, it tells your brain how to behave, what to believe, and how to think and feel. All the elements of successfully creating the reality you want! Second, it helps you set boundaries — the yes's and no's of life. Boundaries are not breached by the people around us: *we* break down our boundaries and let toxic things and people in. By setting your standards of excellence, you'll see your boundaries more clearly so you can hold the line more consistently.

CLARIFYING YOUR GOAT SELF

Grab your GOAT-book. Then follow these steps:

Step 1: Pick a GOAT self to work with

Write at the top of the page the "GOAT self" you want to clarify. Start with whatever you think is easiest — business or career, family, friend — or just create one overarching GOAT. You will repeat this process for each of the "GOAT selves" you want to identify and ultimately live by. Choose the situations that mean the most to you, personally or professionally.

Step 2: Your GOAT behaviors

Now it's blue-sky time! If you could show up as your GOAT self — your BEST self if you prefer — what does that look like? Here are some helpful questions to prompt you to get started, but by all means, go further!

- How do you act?
- How do you think?
- How do you feel?
- What do you say "yes" to and what do you say "no" to?
- What does "success" look like to this version of you?
    - Is it money? (Side note, it's okay to want money, just don't make it the only thing you care about.)
    - A feeling?
    - A state of a relationship? (i.e., no fighting, open communication, etc.)
- Whom do you let in and whom do you keep out?
- Whom or what do you need more or less of?
- How do you sound? Stand? Gesture?
- How do you improve yourself? Do you read?
- Create a group of people you use as sounding boards (if so, who's in the group?).
- What feedback do you need or want?
- How will you measure your progress?
- What time, or how much time, do you devote here?
- How do you know you're being "present" with this GOAT self?
- If this is business, how do you deal with industry pressures?
- If this is your career, how do you handle office politics so that they don't get in your way?

These questions should get you going, but the objective is that by the time you're done, you have a crystal clear idea of the person you want to become, and *you are the one to define that person.* No one else gets the pen unless you give it to them. So, if you've lived your life handing your pens to others to tell you what to do and how, it's time to take them all back. Collect the pens. Thank them for their contribution and throw those pens in the fire. There should be only one pen in the entire world that has the power to dictate how to live: *Yours!*

I encourage you to put down this book and do this exercise. Sure, you might say, "*I'll get to that later,*" but who is that talking, really? Your Dragon, in case you hadn't guessed. Doing something "later" is the Dragon's favorite phrase to make sure you avoid hard but important work. Procrastinating is a symptom of low self-worth, so practice valuing yourself at a higher level now by doing this work. Start with one. You can go from there.

Don't worry. I'll wait. (Imagine me humming to myself as you do your work).

MY PERSONAL BEST CHEAT SHEET

Welcome back! I know you've been working your butt off, creating your GOAT-y world. I hope you're finding this as much fun and inspiring as I did. You're inspiring yourself, my friend! Get used to it.

These definitions are great, but you have to remind yourself to keep following your own rule book. I created a simple cheat sheet, which you can download with every other worksheet here at www.dragonandgoatbook.com. There are five simple questions to ask yourself, preferably once a week. I suggest you put a fifteen-minute meeting in your calendar on whatever day is best to do this task. Go ahead. Do it now. As you can see, I'm a very patient little book.

Now that your *commitment is in your calendar,* here are the five questions to keep you strong and firm in your GOAT-ness:

1. I think like this about myself and my business and its future …
2. The work I consistently focus on is …
3. I take care of myself in these ways …
4. The metrics I hold myself accountable for are …
5. I'll know I'm successful because …

These five questions take you from checking in with your feelings, to the work you're doing (productive, not busy!), your self-care through to incrementally checking your progress and success. Going over these each week creates a habit of assessing your life, happiness, and success. The process of reviewing is more important than planning, because it allows you to see where you are progressing, where you're stuck, and if you've fallen behind in your commitments to yourself and your GOAT-ness.

When you write the book of your own life, you get to decide the chapters and the ending. Don't give anyone else that right.

To be a GOAT, you have to live a GOAT life, and the first step is to define what that GOAT life *is!*

CREATING YOUR PURPOSE STATEMENT

Once you have your GOAT self/selves nicely defined, it's time to give it purpose. You hear about living a "purpose-driven life"; but it's hard to know how to *do* that. How do you find your "purpose"? Is it hiding under a bush? In a tree? Under your bed?

Thankfully for you, I've sourced a great way not only to create this amazing purpose statement but also to make it something you can live by and remember. I use mine as a guide to the work I do, the clients I take on, the people I surround myself with, and how I behave every day. It's an all-for-one deal!

There are three parts to creating a purpose statement to guide your GOAT self through life. But one note before we go further: This statement is not a tagline or marketing slogan. It doesn't appear on your website or business cards. This is something you write in your mind and heart. It's personal, and it will change as you do more, grow, and evolve yourself. At the end, we'll piece all three sections together into a nice, neat (but not necessarily short) statement. I got this process from Brendon Burchard when I went through my certification training, and I've used it religiously ever since.

Step 1: Make it personal

The first part of your statement is to remind you of how you want to BE. This stage is meant to be internally focused. Write down words or phrases that relate only to YOU and what YOU can control about your behavior. Things like being present, kind, thoughtful, open, curious, inventive, learning, growing, happy, content, calm, confident, and so on.

Grab that GOAT-book and write down a few words that resonate with you.

Step 2: It's about interactions

This is the step where you identify how you want to interact with *others*. These words or short phrases are relationship-based and define how you want people to feel when they're with you. Things like trustworthy, asking good questions, mentor, inspirational, motivating, challenging, teaching, caring, helping, guiding, and so on.

Write down some words or phrases that work for you here.

Step 3: The "so that"

This part is not a "so what." It's a "so that" or the outcome of the work you do by BEING and ACTING as you stated above. What happens? How do you want your legacy to be remembered? When someone works with you, how are their lives better because you were there? Think hard about this one. This is primarily what will guide you most in the work you do and the people you do that work with. It will also determine your relationships on the personal side.

Examples of "so thats" are:

- Here's mine: … So that I can help people live happier, wealthier and more fulfilled lives
- Other examples:
  - … So that people know that they will always be cared for
  - … So that after every transaction, they know they made the best decision of their lives
  - … So that I am living my GOAT-ness 100% of the time, no compromises

The inspiration for my "so that" was based on my Dark Side, that part of me I never want to go back to. I spent too many years feeling miserable and poor. I felt like nothing I did mattered. I often wondered if I'd be missed if I just disappeared. Those feelings were so strong, and so devastating, that I dedicate my life and my work to preventing anyone from getting to that level of pain.

There is no right or wrong way to do the "so that" part. It just comes down to the overall outcome you are striving to achieve. This last section should be your guide, and as you review the work you do, you have to ask yourself, *"Am I living up to my purpose?"* I took my on-demand video courses offline and stopped doing them because they weren't achieving any of the outcomes I wanted. They weren't making anyone wealthy, and I'm pretty sure the client's credit card bills didn't make them feel fulfilled, knowing they paid for something they didn't use.

I've measured my relationships, partnerships, and projects against my "so that" yard stick. Before I do anything, I ask if it will make people happier, wealthier, or more fulfilled. If the answer is "no," then it's not for my GOAT self and I don't proceed. It's for my old self, and I don't want to be that person anymore.

Step 4: Bringing it all together

To complete the purpose statement, you take Steps 1–3 and string them together into one (sometimes long, but no one is judging you) sentence!

Here's how it will sound:

> *The purpose of my life is to BE (step 1 stuff), to ACT/ INTERACT (step 2 stuff) so that (step 3 stuff).*

Mine sounds like this:

> *The purpose of my life is to be present, curious, and always focused on my personal growth, to ask really good questions to lead my clients to their GOAT selves so that I can help them lead happier, wealthier, and more fulfilled lives.*

What's yours? Get your GOAT-book and start writing. I'll wait. I'll go get a snack while you do your work. Feel free to refer to the resources on www.dragonandgoatbook.com if you need some help. Be back in a minute!

IMPACT OVER INCOME – THE STRATEGY

Now that your GOAT standards have been set and your purpose is in place, it's time to talk about moving from a fear-based, income-driven life to a GOAT-driven, impact-focused one. You've already read about my income to impact journey. Now I'm going to give you the steps so you can get there too.

For as long as I can remember, I've been scared stiff. Scared of letting people down, not living up to expectations, not making enough money, not keeping a job or doing it well, not having what it takes to be "successful," and so on. It didn't matter how much money I made with my agency, I still worried daily about where my next client was going to come from, how much money I'd made that month, and was I even in the black. If I was successful one month, I'd instantly worry about the next.

When I finally decided that my agency had to go, I knew it would take more than just going from running one company to another. I had to change what *drove me*. I couldn't go through the fear-cycle I'd been stuck in. I wanted to focus on doing really good work, and in so doing, attract more clients and grow my business. The change sounds simple, but it will fight your Dragon *hard*.

The way I used to run my business was this:

INCOME (WHERE ARE MY CLIENTS?)

IMPACT (I'LL DO GOOD WORK FOR THEM)

I just focused on butts in seats, client counts, and revenue. It sounds shallow, but when you've spent years kiting credit cards and wallowing in crippling debt, having blown up your life without real life skills and with two small boys to feed, it's understandable. I've forgiven myself for this money-based focus because at the time, it was all I knew. But fear was my driver, constantly nipping at my heels.

When I switched to coaching, I wasn't that scaredy-cat anymore, but breaking that habit seemed impossible. To make my performance coaching practice really rock and roll, I had to change the equation:

IMPACT (I'LL DO MY ABSOLUTE BEST WORK)

INCOME (THE MONEY COMES BECAUSE MY CLIENTS' RESULTS ROCK)

This new phase was all about believing that my work would be good enough to bring in the business. And that terrified me. I would clutch the edge of my desk and repeat the phrase "impact over income" over and over again. I said it so I'd believe it. My Dragon gave me every reason to think I was nuts. No one does this. You'll run out of money. It will never work. You're making Marc carry the household AGAIN. The doubts rolled in, day after day.

Eventually, it worked. This change in mindset and practice has generated the most amazing life for me. I never worry about where my clients will come from. I trust in my ability to figure it out and do the work. I launched my practice on March 3, 2020— right when the world shut down with the pandemic. I couldn't have picked a worse time, really. But to me, people still needed what I had — they were just a little harder to find now.

My preferred GOAT-based choice to get clients is doing work-shops. They watch me, and if they like what they see, they book time in my calendar. Since the pandemic had everyone running scared, hoarding toilet paper and water, getting their attention was going to be tough. So, instead of doing one event a month, I did two a week. I didn't panic. I knew that if I demonstrated what I knew, people would come. I didn't run crazy ads or do anything *other than what I loved to do*. I just did more of it.

It worked. Within six months, I was running a six-figure company. The following year, I doubled it. The year after that, I was up 50% yet again. I make more on my bottom line now than ever before. With my agency, my profit was about 5%. My profit margin with my coaching practice is close to 80%. With my new business, I can earn a lot less revenue but make a lot more profit. Anyone can brag about running a "million-dollar company," but that doesn't mean they're profitable.

Now that you can see how it's done and that it works (and not just for me but for my clients too), let's get you on that same GOAT track.

Step 1: What fear do you have to release?

To make the switch from income-driven living to impact-focused work, you have to face your fears. The first step is to name them. What are you really afraid of? The most common fears can include:

- Running out of money
- Where your clients/deals are coming from next
- Paying bills (personal and professional)
- Falling behind vs. your competitors or peers
- Not achieving your goals

What are yours? Write them down, because when you do, you bring them out of the darkness within, and into the light. They're a lot less scary that way.

Step 2: What impact do you want to have?

Like your purpose statement, your impact determines the type of work you should be doing. How are people's lives better? What does "doing great work" sound like to you? How will your amazing work attract more people or projects, and therefore achieve the income and credibility you desire?

Being referred is about being remembered. Being promoted is about delivering consistent value and playing your political cards properly. If you do great work, people talk about you. If you could tell them, what would you want them to say? How would they define your work? Your brand is not what you say about your work; it's what *others* say about you.

Step 3: Do the work

What actual tasks and actions will you need to take in order to make that impact a reality? List them so it's easy for you to execute every day. They're your impact-generating instructions. There's not much to this step other than doing the work. It might scare you to do away with work that isn't impactful, even if you're good at it. I'm good at online courses, but I'm not doing them. They don't generate the outcome I want for my clients. I can busy myself with those courses, and it will fill my days nicely. But my return on my time invested is negative.

Schedule into your calendar specific times to do your main, most impactful tasks. Put them on repeat often. This is practicing and living your GOAT life, so, get 'er done!

FOSTERING A GROWTH MINDSET

We all have fixed mindsets, but those that make it hard for you to live a GOAT life have to go. My bad memory fixed mindset made going to the grocery store problematic if I didn't have a list, but it didn't kill my business. My fixed mindset about being second-rate and perpetually unsuccessful did. That one had to go.

The process of switching from a fixed to a growth mindset is similar to the From Filth to Fertilizer process: you start with a fixed set of beliefs, then ask yourself if there is a different way of looking at it. Where the two processes differ is the From Filth to Fertilizer process deals with past traumas or situations you continue to drag through your life. Switching from a fixed to a growth mindset is about internally living and leading with the desire to learn. Fixed mindset people look at the world as deterministic: it is what it is and nothing will change. Growth mindset individuals view the world as a place of choice, free will, and expansion.

How to make the switch

As with anything, awareness is key! The first step is to clarify and define your fixed mindsets — the areas in your life viewed as "can't or won't change it." Then, challenge yourself to come up with a more growth-oriented way of looking at things.

Get your GOAT-book out so you can write down the ones that trigger your need to change mindsets and then keep going with more of your own examples!

Fixed: I'm not good at (name that thing).
Growth: I am untrained at (that thing).

Fixed: People say they're giving me "feedback," but they're really criticizing me
Growth: Feedback helps me learn. I can take or leave any advice, as I see fit.

Fixed: I'm too shy to speak in front of people
Growth: With practice, I can become confident at speaking anywhere!

Fixed: They're just naturally smart and successful. They were born that way. I'm not.
Growth: No one is "born" any way. With effort, practice, and persistence, anything can be mastered!

Fixed: When other people succeed, I feel bad about myself.
Growth: Hooray for them! They can inspire me on my own path!

Fixed: They're just lucky.
Growth: Luck is practice and opportunity and training my brain to see all of the good things around me so I'm ready when they appear!

Fixed: I hate making mistakes. I look stupid.
Growth: It's just testing. If something didn't work, I'll put it aside and try something else.

Fixed: Failure means it's time to give up.
Growth: Failure is taking something that didn't work personally — and it's time to get my creative juices going and find something new, or invest more time to see this through.

Fixed: I can't do that!
Growth: I can't do that … YET.

That last one is my favorite because it's so easy. The "I can't" reflex is a big one and applies to so many situations and circum-stances. But add the word "yet" to the end of it, and now you've got something to work with! Take away the help-lessness and powerlessness of a fixed mindset and replace it with control. You have more control over your life and your world than you think, but fixed mindsets will blind you to the possibilities. GOATs see everything as a growth opportunity. So, get your GOAT on and fix those mindsets!

CONFIDENCE & MOTIVATION COME AFTER ACTION

I know far too many people who wait to feel a certain way before they do something. These feelings are things like:

- Courage
- Bravery
- Confidence
- Being ready
- Motivation
- Knowing our passions

The sad truth is that if you're waiting to feel these things, you'll be waiting a long, long time. They'll never come because, as GOATs know, these emotions come *after* we've started moving toward our goals.

You feel brave *after* you've done something courageous. You feel ready *after* you've started down a new path.

You feel motivated *after* you've taken even the smallest of steps toward something meaningful.

You find your passions *after* you've tried a bunch of things and narrowed down your options to the things that bring you joy and satisfaction.

There is a large crowd standing at the bus stop, waiting for these emotions to show up. They feel comfortable hanging around because they're not alone. Everyone is waiting! Look at us waiting together! They must know something because they wouldn't be here if the feelings never showed up, right? Wrong. Do the important work, and those reassuring emotions will come, giving you the added strength to keep going.

There are two simple steps to overcome this problem.

Step 1: What are you waiting for, really?

Get your GOAT-book out. Think of something you have hesitated to start, stop, or investigate. What's *really* going on? What are you waiting for? What feeling do you want to experience before you can start down this path? Write down whatever feelings you think you need such as readiness, confidence, courage, motivation, and so on. Go to a thesaurus and look up other words if you want. I do that all the time! Go through the Emotion Wheel: Do any words pop out at you?

Step 2: Taking small steps

I'm not a "massive action" kind of girl. I'm more the "Snoopy Shuffle" kid. Small steps will eventually lead to big results, so don't think you have to kill yourself to get what you want. What are your next small steps, however tiny? Write down all the actions, steps, calls, conversations, reports, presentations, emails, texts, strategies, Word docs, spreadsheets, lists, and so on that apply.

I was scared to start Masterminds out of fear that no one would come, and I hate selling. These two fears stopped me for a long time. But when I decided it was time to get on the horse, I mapped out every tiny little thing that had to be done, and I picked the easiest one to start with. Then I just went from there. Succeeding in the small things gave me courage and confidence to take on bigger and bigger challenges.

Make your list of actions small enough for your brain to say, *"I can do that,"* and you'll feel all the emotions you need to gain all the strength and resolve you need. GOATs take small steps; they don't leap buildings in a single bound. They climb a mountain starting from the bottom and carefully make their way up. So, start walking up that mountain, head down, doing the work, believing in the outcomes. Then, a little ways up, lift your head and marvel at just how far you've come. It's a wonderful feeling.

FROM GOALS TO ACTIONS – REPLACE DECISIONS WITH INSTRUCTIONS

Decision fatigue is a horrible, daily problem for most people. When we wake up each day, our brains are at full operating capacity. But as soon as we start making decisions — what to wear, eat for breakfast, the music we play on the way to work — our brain's capacity starts to deplete.

If you force your brain to make too many decisions, by about 2:00 pm, you're out of juice. Your brain feels foggy, you want to take a nap, your decisions become more haphazard, you can get short with people, or just "do it yourself" instead of giving the task to someone else. Decision fatigue leads to poor decision making, rash behavior, and impulse buying. By 5:00 pm, you have so little patience that someone asking you "What's for dinner?" can send you into a volcanic rage. So how do you protect your brain from this foggy, overreacting disaster? The answer is simple: give yourself instructions.

Steve Jobs wore the same thing every day to avoid decision fatigue. So did Mark Zuckerberg. Most GOATs have created routines and structures for their days so they barely have to think about it. My morning routine is exactly the same every day: get up, brush teeth (etc.), have breakfast, go to the gym with Marc, come home and have tea/coffee in the backyard (on the couch during our Canadian winters), shower, and head to work. My meals and workouts are pre-planned, so I just show up and go. I shop on Sundays, and do meal prep. I lay out my workout stuff the night before. I basically make zero decisions before 9:30 am, which sets me up for an amazing day.

In this section, you will have a few strategies to choose from to reduce decisions and increase your brainpower throughout the day. Pick the one that your brain resists the least and start small.

The art of little chunking

I love little chunking. It started with Mel, who was freaked out by big goals. They felt unattainable, so we broke them down into "I can do that" chunks. Hence, "little chunking." This process worked so well that I actually created a day planner for it. You can get a copy of the one-sheet on the www.dragonandgoatbook.com.

The process goes like this:

Step 1: Annual goals

What is your annual goal? Think of what you want to achieve by the end of the year. It can be monetary, the number of clients, a health goal, and so on.

Step 2: Quarterly objectives

Split the year into four quarters, then assign each quarter an objective. These don't have to be concrete. They can be things like launching a marketing system, hiring five people, making $X amount of money, creating a team system, or getting yourself organized. Each should be aligned with your annual goal. If you achieve these four objectives, you'll naturally hit your annual goal without effort.

Step 3: Monthly targets

Now we're getting specific. Take each quarter and split them into three months. Then, assign three measurable, verifiable actions/ targets for each month. You can repeat the targets for each if that works. For instance, you can set a target of each month recruiting four new people. Or if your business is seasonal or cyclical, you can vary the number a bit. Launch a campaign. Lose 5 lbs. Go on vacation for at least one day to take a break. Book a certain specific number of meetings. Host two workshops. Targets are "yes/no" tasks and are your most important business and career building tasks. By the end of the month, it would be 100% clear that you did, or did not, achieve those targets.

By focusing on achieving smaller targets each month, for three months straight, you'll easily hit your quarterly objective. If you do that three more times in the year, you naturally will hit your annual goal. It always just rolls up. But we're not done yet.

Step 4: Weekly tasks

We're going to break down each month into weeks, making the tasks more doable and creating an environment where you're less prone to give up or become overwhelmed. To hit those monthly targets, you now need to assign yourself tasks each week to get the work done. This is where you really get into avoiding decision fatigue and convert your days to following instructions!

If your monthly target is to get four new recruits or make $X, then what do you have to do to make it happen? Do you need to make X number of calls — write down the actual names of the people you will call. Will you send emails out? Itemize who's going to be getting them and what you're going to say in these emails. Shooting videos? What's the topic, and when will you shoot and post it? You see how this works: whether you take people for lunch, write a report, offer a workshop/webinar, or host an event, make a list of the tasks that support the monthly targets and then *put that in your calendar*. With greater specificity on the tasks, the fewer decisions you have to make, and you reduce the likelihood of avoiding the work.

To repeat a well-loved, slightly ass-kicking phrase: commitment or cowardice show up in the calendar! I like to review my work each Sunday, looking ahead to see what my week looks like. How many meetings do I have? What's coming up that I need to prepare for?

Then I check my to-do list to see what I can advance by putting time blocks into the gaps. I challenge myself to see if there are any non-GOAT tasks and eliminate any that have crept in. This routine sets the tone for my week and makes me feel in control of my time and my energy.

At the end of each day, I review what I have done. Did I accomplish what I had set out to do? What got in my way? What can I move to tomorrow or the next slot? Sometimes weekends are my only option. But I make sure to protect most of my weekends for fun time. If I have to do work, it should be before people are up, or when nothing is going on.

The act of reviewing your workweek is key to the system's success, so don't skip it. Never let your week or day get away from you. If they do, have a routine to bring everything back under control. GOATs reduce decision making to *only* the most important things. Negotiations. Business or career growth. Inventing new strategies. Building stronger relationships. Being super intentional with their time. You can't be intentional if you're trying to wing your way through the day. It won't work. It might for a time, but GOATs know that overwhelm and burnout are just around the corner.

Try this exercise now. Get out your GOAT-book or download the worksheet at www.dragonandgoatbook.com and jot down information in each of the four steps, breaking it down as you go into smaller and smaller, more manageable chunks.

The GOAT life is mostly decision-free because your brain needs to be at its best to build the life, business, career, or relationships that fulfill you the most.

Rearview mirror goal setting

Not everyone loves goals. So, while the little chunking method-ology is awesome for some, it can be downright distressing for others. In this case, I recommend what I call "rearview mirror" goal setting. I credit Leon with helping me come up with this. In my GOAT Mastermind, the group was to assign themselves a task that would grow their business, and then set a deadline. Every single time, Leon deflected, asking to go last as we discussed everyone's goals. And every time I came to him, he never, ever set a goal. Before I started making the assumption that he was stonewalling, I asked him, how *did* he set goals?

His answer changed my perspective on goals forever. He stated that he prefers to look at where he is today and back at a certain time interval — say a month — and assess how much incremental progress he has made. If it's not enough, he scales up his effort. If he's on target, he continues at his current pace. And if he's ahead of the game, well, he'll probably work to beat his own high score next month!

The premise behind this is sound: when you set goals, eventually you "win"; and instead of setting a new goal, you may start to coast. You did it! You're done! The game is over! I've worked with many clients who stall out for this exact reason. But if you want to *stay in the game*, then you'll have to adopt the rearview mirror approach. This means the game never ends, but you can always be winning. Leon hates it when games end. He gets bored. That's why this works so well for him.

Here's how to execute your rearview mirror process:

Step 1: Pick your metric

What will you be measuring? It has to be connected with your GOAT work, or it won't advance your GOAT life. The metric you're looking for also needs to be tied to the results you want to achieve. Be specific and make sure it's easy to identify whether you're winning or losing at your game.

Step 2: Pick your time interval

What time interval will you use to measure yourself? A month, a quarter, a week? Pick the interval that allows you enough time to get the GOAT work done and see results. If your timeline is too short, you won't see patterns. You can have a mix-and-match approach to this too. If you like short intervals, that's fine. Just add in a longer-term interval as well so that you're always getting a higher-level view of your business and can see the overall trajectories instead of just what's happening right now. A good business or career manages both short-and long-term intervals.

Step 3: What will you do?

What action will you take if your results aren't as high as you want? Make sure you have a plan. It removes decisions, guesswork, and anxiety. If you take the right actions, should your results slow or go negative, it's pure execution. You may have to increase the frequency of action, change a behavior, or add another task to the mix. It's just logistics, as I like to say. Your Dragon won't see these instructions as a threat, so it stays out of your way.

GOATs choose the goal setting, self-motivating system that works best for them, and I encourage you to do the same. You can merge little chunking with the rearview mirror process. Adjust them until it works for you.

And then it's just logistics!

SETTING BOUNDARIES — OKAY AND NOT OKAY

We can set our boundaries, but we cannot blame others for breaking through them. We let them. GOATs protect their boundaries, strengthening them not because they are stubborn or obstinate but because they know when to say "yes" or "no."

Kim, a beloved client with a heart of pure gold, struggled with some of the people in her life. She had spent a life striving harder than anyone I know to live up to heavy, almost cruel expectations. Time and time again, she'd let these toxic people in, and every time they'd twist her words, crushing her soul. But she loved them and felt that one day they would see her beauty and value. Except they didn't. Over time, Kim came to realize that what she wanted from them, they were unable to give. This created an immense sadness because in choosing to let go of her hopes for what she wanted from others, she began to grieve. It feels like a death, only we have living reminders that they're still here, compounding the conflicted feelings within.

But Kim decided to set her boundaries. She stopped accepting their inconsistent offerings and cruel jabs and started setting down terms. She decided when they can and cannot talk with her. What they can and cannot say. Things she won't accept anymore. She stopped going to functions with a history of making her feel small. She created space for herself by adding distance between those who weren't living up to her expectations of kindness. They were not removed from her life, but there was a new flavor to their interaction. It was on *her* terms now, not theirs. It was at this point that her healing began and the grief began to lift. She had set her boundaries, and now she was safe. The only task now was to keep them protected.

The boundaries we set in our lives keep us in control. It doesn't create an island effect — you're not *alone*. You are simply the only one with hands on the controls. When you let toxic or negative people into your world, they get to push buttons on the control panel of your life, and it can be catastrophic. They can crash you. They can tilt your world. And then it's a fight to get it back on track.

Look at them more like passengers, not co-pilots. As audience members and not the cast. And if they don't support your path or vision, or even just remain neutral, remove them or create distance and space between your interactions. Setting and holding boundaries is connected deeply with setting your own terms and writing your own story, as we've seen. But I felt that this particular issue was so pressing that it deserved its own section and some strategic steps so you can begin to build or strengthen the boundaries in your life.

Without them, you run the risk of being exploited or taken advantage of, giving too much without receiving anything back, feeling resentful and bitter, and massively disrespected and small.

It's time to get out the GOAT-book!

Step 1: Who and what needs boundaries?

Brené Brown says that "Clear is kind; unclear is unkind," so we're going to start with being clear and kind to yourself. Before you can talk about boundaries, you need to set them. Then, the more you talk about your boundaries, the more they will be respected. If no one knows there are limits, then they will walk right through them. That's not their fault; they didn't know, and it's time to change that.

Think about what you need to set boundaries around and write down the ones that need limits. Things like:

- Time
- Energy
- Effort
- Personal space
- Social media

- The news
- Events
- Add to this list if you have more!

There may also be people for whom you need to set limits, so write this list too. People like:

- Extended family
- Friends
- Romantic partners
- Kids
- Coworkers
- Clients
- Bosses/subordinates
- Even strangers!

Step 2: Identify what boundaries need to be set

Make your boundaries clear and concrete. You will need to communicate them clearly and repeatedly. If you don't know how to explain them, no one else will respect them. People do not know what you want, so in case you're holding out for them to telepathically "know what you need," it's not happening. Let that thought go. It's time to express yourself! But first, we have to know what we're talking about.

Here are some sample questions when starting to set more clear boundaries:

- What is causing me unnecessary stress or discomfort?
- What do I look forward to each day versus what do I dread?
- Who or what gives me energy?
- What areas of my life do I feel exhausted by?
- What makes me feel safe, supported, and valued?[10]

---

10 www.scienceofpeople.com/how-to-set-boundaries

This will begin to put structure around where your boundaries need to be set. Sometimes to set boundaries, we start with what makes us safe and then move to the other side and identify what makes us feel unsafe or depletes our energy.

Open your GOAT-book so you have two blank pages. Draw a big circle on each side. In one circle, write all the things that make you feel safe. Examples include:

- A daily routine
- Words of affirmation or certain acts of kindness from your partner
- Hugs from your loved ones
- Leaving work stress in the office
- Clear communication from your loved ones
- Freedom to decide how you spend your free time
- Saying "no" to energy vampires
- Autonomy over your body

Then, in the other circle, write all the things that make you feel unsafe or taken advantage of. Things like:

- Your parents telling you what to do with your life
- Working after-hours or weekends on projects instead of prioritizing self-care
- Worrying about what certain people think about you
- Your cousin asking to borrow money
- Your coworker constantly dumping her relationship problems on you at lunch
- Your roommate eating your food from the fridge
- Your significant other or parents controlling who you talk to or hang out with
- Strange people at the bar touching you without asking
- Acquaintances asking deep or intimate questions about your life

Create as big of a list as you need. These are your limits, things you do not want to accept in your life. And it's okay to set these boundaries. You are not being mean. You are not being unkind. You don't hate people; you love yourself enough to set these limits so that no one takes away your love, your joy, and your passion for life.

Step 3: Communicating your boundaries

Whooooo boy. This is the part most people dread. How do you tell people about your newly created limits when you've never done it before?

Here are some helpful tips sourced from www.scienceofpeople. com:

Time Boundary	"I can only stay for an hour" or "If you're going to be late, please let me know ahead of time."
Energy Boundary	"I don't have the energy to help you with [their request] right now, but maybe [this resource] can help."
Emotional Dumping	"I understand you're having a hard time and I want to be there for you, but I don't have the emotional capacity to listen right now."
Personal Space Boundary	"It makes me feel uncomfortable when you [touch or action]. If you can't respect my space, I'll have to leave."
Conversational Boundary	"This is not a topic I'm willing to discuss right now."
Comment Boundary	"I don't find those types of comments funny."
Mental Boundary	"I understand we see things differently, and I respect your opinion, but please don't force it on me."
Material Boundary	"Please ask me first before borrowing my [possession]," or "I would appreciate it if you didn't touch my [material thing]."
Social Media Boundary	"I don't feel comfortable with you posting that on Instagram."

www.scienceofpeople.com/how-to-set-boundaries.

Communicating what you want can be done with grace and kindness. It doesn't have to be a confrontation. But it *is* about stepping up and standing up for yourself. People are three times more likely than you think to say "yes" to you and accept what you ask of them. But you'll never know if support is there until you make the effort. It's okay to ask for what you want. It's okay to step away if something is overwhelming, or you're just done. It happens to me all the time. But because I explain my limits to others, they never take it personally, and our relationships are stronger than ever.

Step 4: Reiterating and standing your ground

Now that you have your boundaries and have communicated them, it's time to protect the ramparts! Hold the line! Keep protecting your GOAT life! Keeping up your boundaries protects your health, well-being, passion for life, and your GOAT-ness.

Sometimes, despite the fact that you communicated your boundaries to others, they're not used to those limits and may cross them. Just reiterate them again, calmly but firmly. Do not make concessions because then you've broken a boundary.

If someone is uncomfortable, do not shift your limits to make them feel better. They won't anyway. Their discomfort is not about you. And don't be afraid to say "No." You don't have to apologize, explain, or justify your boundaries by describing the reasons behind the "no." It's just "no." The more time you spend with "no," the better you'll feel about it. Some people will ask some-thing of me, and when my answer is "no," they begin to apologize. I reaffirm that they can ask any question they like! It's just that the answer is "no," and we move on without hurt feelings or resentment.

Your GOAT needs protection, and you can deliver it with grace and kindness but without compromise.

SUPERPOWERS AND DARK SIDES

Two things that GOATs are really good at acknowledging and accepting are their superpowers and their dark side. Superpowers are your unique talents — the things you're really good at that few others can match. The things that come easily to you, while others have to study and strive to get even half as good at them as you are. And they're really, really hard to define, mostly because we're not taught to stand out. We're taught to fit in and conform. Do and be like everyone else. Stand out a little, just not too much. We talked about this in the Dragon part of the book, so no need to revisit those nightmares!

My superpower is driven primarily by how my brain is wired. My autistic brain is specially designed to detect patterns and retain information in an almost photographic way (just not grocery lists, those I forget all the time). I then have the unique ability to bring together what I'm hearing with strategies and solutions that fit the situation my client is experiencing, and voila! A great business, amazing results for my clients, and the feeling that I'm doing my GOAT work.

Ashley, my dear friend, asked me one day, *"If you had to describe me in one word, what would it be and why?"* She was being nominated for Broker of the Month and couldn't come up with the word. To me, it was clear within seconds: devotion.

Ashley's superpower is devotion: to her craft, her people, her friends, her community, and anyone else she can help, including perfect strangers. The first word that cropped up for me was "dedicated," but she throws so much emotion and feeling into her work that the word had to be stronger, and "devotion" fit the bill.

When she's devoted to something, there is nothing that will stop her from seeing it through. I have lots of clients who work hard and do amazing things. Ashley's approach just has a different *feeling* to it. A deeper connection. A desire for everyone to get the best outcome — including herself. Why not? She's a savvy businesswoman with a life to lead and fun to be had!

There's a difference between "talent" and "skills." Ashley's talent is her devotion. Her skills are how she runs her real estate brokerage, sets up her systems, recruits and trains her team and staff, and how she manages her time. She does the hard work and gets rid of things that take her away from getting to the work she is devoted to.

My talent is noticing patterns and connecting clients with strategies that allow them to find their GOAT-ness. My skills are asking really good questions, researching new methodologies, presenting them in a way that makes sense to people, and showing folks how to measure their progress.

It's your turn now. Get out that GOAT-book. You'll want it for this part!

Step 1: Defining your superpowers

Your superpower is your own special talent. When you do super-power work, everything else falls into place, effortlessly. Some examples of talents I've helped people to see include:

- Organization by taking a chaotic office, team, group, or organization and creating systems, processes, and routines to remove decisions and add fulfillment and effortlessness
- Creating operational systems that support an organization and teaching people how to implement them, eventually without their support
- Connecting emotionally with an audience in a way that not only motivates but creates action
- Identifying an entrepreneur's unique opportunity to scale their business, either through marketing, sales, partnership opportunities, and more
- Working with people, managing confrontations so everyone gets what they want
- Negotiating deals, solving problems on the fly, and getting to the end result everyone's happy with

What's your talent? What's your "thing," even if you're not doing it right now? This is not easy. Maybe, like Ashley, you need to ask someone to help you see it. When I do leadership training, I like to ask the group, "What talent do you bring to the table that's going to contribute to the company's growth?" I did this once, and five out of ten people had no answer. So, the rest of the group told them what *they* thought these five people contributed to the group. For those who struggled to see their value, the outside perspective offered a clearer vision. Use whatever resources you need, but you have to identify your talents.

Next up are the skills you need to practice to hone your talents and make this process the primary part of the work you do!

Step 2: What skills do you need?

Now that you have your talent figured out, it's time to focus on the skills you need to master to make it easier to use that magical part of you. At a recent workshop, a woman declared "organization" as being her superpower. Her skills were to build smooth systems at work, problem solve, research new methodologies and solutions, and learn how to improve her communication skills so more people get on board with her ideas. When she created these new organizational masterpieces, people actually understood and used them!

For Steven and his consulting practice, his talent is taking complex back-end operational systems and simplifying them for others to install. He had to hone his skills in communication, researching new processes to continue to evolve and improve his offering, and ask coaching questions to help his clients implement solutions.

In your GOAT-book, write down the supporting skills you need to perfect to make more space for your talent. But there's a difference between improving skills and pointless instruction. GOATs avoid endlessly educating themselves to fill up their calendars, particularly in areas that aren't necessary for their super-power development. A full calendar does not always equate to a full bank account. They learn, but they don't take a zillion classes, hoping to one day "have all the answers."

As you work on your skills, make sure you keep track of how it improves your overall performance. Add your skills tasks to your calendar, your Little Chunking tool, or the way you measure progress through the Rearview Mirror process. Track your results and adjust as needed. It's the premise behind becoming 1% better: just pick one skill and ask yourself how you can become 1% better at it today? Over time, this approach will get you everything you want.

Stick to your GOAT path. Gear up your superpowers because we're about to go to the dark side …

THE DARK SIDE

We all have a dark side, a feeling or situation that you never want to experience again. We cannot get rid of these dark moments because they *are* us. Mine were dark, grey, and with an unsettling quiet. Not the kind that is calming, but the kind where you know something is going to jump you from behind, and you may or may not make it out this time. But we have to identify this dark part of us because it's either going to sit there and fester and make us bitter, or we can use it for fuel.

My dark side was growing up crushed by rules. The older I got, the more rules there were to follow and the colder and greyer my world became. I lost color in my life. I lost passion. I lost joy. I looked in the mirror one day and wondered if I should just walk away from everything. I didn't know who I was, and it scared me. In those days, I felt helpless, powerless, weak, alone, and terrified. On the outside, I was fine. My anger and sadness had nowhere to go, and no way to feel validated. I watched how other people lived and did the same, as closely as I could. While everyone around me thought that all was well, I knew there was a gaping hole within.

So, I blew everything up. I left the church. Got a divorce. Lost my job. Started over.

Even after those volcanic events and the aftershocks that plagued me for years as I tried to get myself put back together, I was afraid. That fear haunted me day and night, and I felt like I was constantly running, running, running. I'd left my old life behind, but in truth it was still with me in my head and my heart. It has taken me years, using the strategies in this book and the help of wonderful coaches and psychologists, to repair my self-worth and step fully into my super-powers. Today, I don't run on anything but a treadmill, and that rather unwill-ingly. But I remember those dark days, culminating in a rolled car on a six-lane highway, staring at oncoming traffic and hoping they'd stop in time.

My "so that" is to help people feel happy, wealthy, and fulfilled because I spent way too many years feeling miserable and poor, like nothing I did mattered. I strive to improve my talent not only to stay away from the darkness but to guide as many others to see the power of their own dark sides, to take away its sting, venom, and power.

Get your GOAT-book out and take some time to examine your dark side. What do you want to never experience or feel again? Defining this can be difficult because you're looking at something painful. But if you imbue these experiences with purpose, they lose the ability to hurt you. They're *useful* to you now! Liam, one of my clients who loves *Star Wars*, would particularly appreciate this "dark side" part. He's defined his well, and runs his business on helping others heal from their traumas and see their self-worth more clearly. His ability to relate his story to those of his clients builds empathy and inspires him to guide his clients to happier and more successful living.

GOATs know there is good and sad within (not bad — sad). But we can use it to our advantage. Strip your dark side of its power and set your world on fire!

HOW TO GET WORK OFF YOUR PLATE: THE ADORE METHOD

In all likelihood, you're doing too much. The reasons may seem legit: you can do it faster and better as training people takes too long, blah blah blah. While those excuses seem valid, they're masking a desire to be a hero instead of a GOAT. Once you come to terms with that, you're ready to go.

Most high performers become accustomed to doing all the work. They have created identities around being the most capable person in the building, the one everyone depends upon for liter-ally everything. While it may make them feel like a hero, in truth they're heading for Planet Burnout. They will miss opportunities because they're too busy doing the work that one to five other people could do.

It can come down to dollars and cents. Every task or job has an income value, from $15/hr work to $1M in salary. The tasks you're taking on, and their commensurate hourly rate, is ultimately what you're paying yourself. If you want to consider yourself worth $1M, your hourly rate is $500/hr. So, if you're doing something you could pay someone else $15/hr to do, you're effectively paying yourself that much lower salary. You can't grow if you keep yourself back doing work you have no business doing. This is not to devalue jobs that are at the lower end of the income spectrum. The world needs everyone to participate at all levels. The objective is to set the rate *you* want to get paid, and only do the work at that level.

Scott made a great choice when he decided to value his time at $513/hr (not sure where the other $13 came from, but I loved his specificity!). One day, he had to deliver a set of keys to a client, but they lived 1.5 hours away. It had to be done that day, but instead of driving the three-hour round trip, he paid $100 to have someone do it for him.

Before he'd valued his time at $513/hr, he would have absolutely driven those keys himself. Why waste $100? But this time, he thought there might be a better way to spend his time, and he was right. In the three hours that he would have been driving those keys to his client, he got a multi-million dollar listing (which delivers a hefty commission!). So, yup, time well spent!

How many mega deals are you missing because you stubbornly refuse to give up work you have no business doing and that doesn't pay your salary, whatever value you set it at? This is where ADORE comes in!

In a few steps, you will clearly see what work you *should* be doing, what you should immediately get rid of, and how.

Get out the GOAT-book. We're going in!

Step 1: Make a list of everything you do in a week

Most people try to cheat on this one and put down words like "work." That's not how this works. You need to write down the specific tasks, from watering the plants and grocery shopping to admin work, client work, and paying bills. Include things like meetings with clients, your team, superiors, partners, and so on. There is no task too small for this step, and the smaller the task, the better. You'll improve your perspective on just how many "busy" things you do in a week.

This step is particularly helpful if you know you need to hire someone to help, but you're not sure what work they'd take off your plate. This is where you start. Make your list, and be specific.

Step 2: Your GOAT work

Beside the items on the list that *only you can do*, your true GOAT work, put your name. If you have a list of twenty tasks, you should have maybe three to five items with your name on it.

You will be tempted to put your name beside things you don't trust others to do. But *trust* is the issue that needs to be worked on, not the task at hand. If you've given work to people in the past and they've screwed up, go back and review what happened. Did you communicate what a "good job" looked like, instead of assuming they'd somehow read your mind? Did you set clear expectations, deadlines, and outlines as to what you wanted? Did you even give it to the right person or just the closest warm body? Chances are there's an opportunity to get better people to do the work, or you need to step up your communication skills.

Take a deep breath and imagine someone else doing that work competently. Trust that you'll be able to do better at assigning tasks in the future, so the work is done well and up to your expectations. Don't get hung up on the number of tasks that will not have your name beside them. Some things, you won't be able to get off your plate right now. But someday, you will. Having a plan on reallocating your non-GOAT work is where your greatness begins.

Step 3: ADORE the rest!

This is the fun part! Getting the work you don't want to do off your plate for good!

For all the items on your list that aren't assigned to you, give it one of the following letters in this acronym:

A – Automate. Can a system automatically help you to do things like sending emails, automating follow up, and so on? When you book a call with me, you automatically get sent a series of emails to prepare you for it. You can automate bill payments, generate reports, grocery orders, and other time-wasters.

D – Delegate. Do you have a team? Can they take over some of the tasks you're doing? If you hesitate because they don't have your skill set, teach them or send them for training. If you worry about how they'll talk with people, have them shadow you and then get them to take the lead so you can see them in action. If you hesitate to hand non-GOAT work to your team, your emotional attachment to that work may be more the issue, rather than something being wrong with the other individual.

O – Outsource. If you don't have a team, or no one on your team has the bandwidth or capability, find an outsourcing partner. There are partners out there for anything, so take the time to look for the right fit. Later in this book, we'll talk about Star Beginnings and how to hire properly so you can have instant fit — not fits of frustration!

R – Replace. There are times when things need to change. Systems, technology, people, and strategies: they all have to be looked at and questioned as to whether they still work.

E – Eliminate. Some things need to just go. Heave ho, out into the garbage you go. They are old, they don't work, they're dragging you down. Again, it's not just people. It can be archaic systems, routines, and food choices in the kitchen!

As you work through the ADORE process, you'll find that there are abundant options for you to get work off your plate so you can focus on your GOAT-work. Don't mow the lawn if you can pay a kid $15 to do it. Don't pay your bills if you get sucked into a vortex of wasted time on social media. Automate the payment process. Don't drive three hours when you can close a deal instead! You don't know what you've missed while you were doing work someone else should do.

GOATs don't waste their time. They know what to take on and what to ADORE. Now you can do it too!

BEING INTENTIONAL WITH YOUR TIME

GOATs are masters at avoiding distractions, whether at home or at work. They also never feel guilty at work (worrying that the family feels neglected) or with family (checking their watches, feeling like they have to rush back to work). There are lots of ways to be busy, but being productive means doing work with intention and purpose. By now you have your standards of excellence, your purpose, your talents, and skills. You even have ways to structure your day. It's time to ensure that while you're working, your brain isn't in la-la-land. First, let's tackle the difference between busy people and productive people. See how many statements on the "busy" side sound true for you …

Busy	Productive
Always moving, running in a million directions	Intentional with your time, including downtime to refresh and reconnect
A million things on the go	Timed, measurable actions
Reactive — anyone's emergency immediately becomes yours to fix	Proactive — gets ahead of projects, deadlines, and workload
Chaos	Calm
Dragged down by "gotta minute" meetings	Allows for questions but challenges team to solve their own problems
No goals — or vague ones at best. You're just winging it every day	Goals, objectives, Key Performance Indicators, and action plans

No systems	Systems with clear desired outcomes, involving automation where necessary
Database with everyone mashed in	Segmented database
No time	Time is a tool, and it's used wisely

To move more to the right, it takes changing the way you look at yourself and validating your emotions so you know what's driving the chaos and procrastination. Overly "busy" people are emotionally dysregulated; they struggle with self-worth and self-appreciation, and it shows up with winging it through the day, keeping their task list in their heads and then forgetting half of it. Make sure you do the emotion work first. Without it, becoming more productive will remain out of reach.

Time blocking

Intentionality can be mastered with time blocking, but first we have to debunk some of the myths around this incredible time-management strategy. If how you've done it in the past hasn't worked, time blocking is not the problem — it's how you've interpreted it.

My attention span is exactly twenty-two minutes long. After that, this girl needs a break. So I never make my time blocks more than twenty minutes. Your attention may last an hour, but few people can last longer than that *and* be able to think in the same way, creatively, GOAT-ly. Research shows you should take a break every forty-five to fifty minutes to keep your brain in top form. Figure out how long you can really be at your best, and make your time blocks exactly that long.

These blocks of time are for important, business-growing, career-building, relationship-strengthening work only. Elon Musk's time blocks are five minutes long. He just figures out how many five-minute slots the task needs and puts it on his calendar accordingly.

The second myth about time blocking is that you need to stack time blocks in your calendar like Legos. If you can get one to two time blocks per day, every day, you'll double your output. Give yourself a break. Put in only the number of time blocks around your meetings and other obligations that make sense.

The third myth is that you need to set your time blocks at the same time every day. The entrepreneurs who I work with couldn't even begin to do this. No day is ever the same! If you have a fluid, unpredictable schedule, take the time each morning to see what's ahead for the day, and then put your time blocks in accordingly. If some days have zero time blocks for important work, give your-self a break. It's okay! By going through the process each day of reviewing your schedule, this creates the habit that soon becomes a routine you can't live without. It also puts full control of your schedule into your hands, so you can't be distracted and dragged into other people's emergencies.

The last piece of advice for time blocking is to factor in breaks. Without them, you'll exhaust yourself by the end of the day. Naps, breaks, and walks in the woods are vastly underrated. But GOATs take time to refresh, regenerate, and reconnect.

Get out your GOAT-book, and write what you believe your attention span to be. You can even do a test! Find something to work on, and see how long it takes before your brain wanders off. Then, tomorrow, check your calendar and start practicing time blocking like a GOAT!

Distraction management

Once you have your GOAT tasks in appropriately timed blocks, it's time to manage distractions. When I'm on a mission, everything goes off. Phone, social media, email, and so on. If I get distracted, it's game over. I'm hopeless, and my work suffers. Studies have shown that if you have your phone in the room with you, even facedown, it's enough to be a distraction. So, stick it in the hall, give it to someone — whatever you have to do. Just get it away from you! This goes for work and personal life too. There's nothing more disrespectful than having someone pick up their phone or look at their digital watch while you're talking. I just stop and wait, or I'll walk away. Don't do that to people, particularly those relationships that you've cultivated carefully.

If a notification does go off while working, it can take anywhere from three to twenty minutes for your focus to come back. You may brag about being a multi-tasker, but you cannot multi-focus. And focus is everything when it comes to being intentional with your time and performing at your highest level. GOATs don't let things get in the way of important work or people. If necessary, they set up systems and support teams to help them concentrate. Or they turn it all off. I promise you, nothing will catch fire in the twenty minutes you assign to your most productive work.

Get your GOAT-book out. We've got two steps to follow.

Step 1: Identify what distracts you

The first thing is to clearly define your distractions. What drags your attention away? If you're not sure, go through a day and make note of the times when you're working at something, but a distraction catches your attention.

It can be things like:

- Social media
- Notifications of any kind
- Phone ringing
- Text messages
- People interrupting you at work or at home
- Pets walking into your office
- Deliveries
- People dropping by unannounced

There are lots of things that can distract you. I will bet that "notifications" will be at the top. Which brings me to step 2 …

Step 2: Eliminating distractions

Now to get rid of these distractions! If notifications are the culprit, turn them off. If people popping into your office is a challenge, close the door or come up with a system that limits the interruptions, or go somewhere else! You may need to remind people about your distraction rules. That's okay. Speak up for yourself, and the people around you will adjust.

Beside each of the distractions noted, put a solution as to how you're going to eliminate or control that situation better. You might not be able to get it to zero, but you can do better!

GOATs scan their environment for distractions constantly. They're aware of the need to get to their important work and won't let unnecessary interruptions stop them. Particularly if your work is focused on getting insanely good results for your clients, team, or organization, every time you're pulled away means fewer results and less joy in life.

THE POWER OF STAR BEGINNINGS

Hire slow, fire fast. This is an old saying but a good one. Sadly, most people hire when they're desperate and take whatever warm bodies they can find. As we saw earlier, Jeff Bezos did the opposite.

Too often, people compromise when they go to hire. Instead of bringing on the best candidate, they'll:

- Hire friends or family (never works out, impossible to fire)
- Figure "They'll work it out on the job" (they don't)
- Hire someone who has SOME of the things they need (but not all)
- Hire on emotion, not on logic
- Hire under pressure from someone else (Uncle Bob wants a favor)

In nearly all these cases, the process fails; the person lasts two weeks, or worse, you keep them on because of guilt, too nervous to fire them. The thing is, they probably *know* they're not right for the job but don't know what to do. And so, you hit a stalemate. You end up with uncomfortable or even combative meetings, and nothing gets done but everyone feels bad.

If there's one area of your business that should never be compromised, it's in bringing on new people: staff, team members, partners, outsourcing companies, and so on.

If you want to change this and take full advantage of the ADORE process, try practicing Star Beginnings.

Step 1: Identify the position and what it will entail

A simple but clear job description, full of tasks to be done, expectations, and obligations is where to begin. If you have someone in the position now, ask them to describe what they're doing. I did this when my operations manager was leaving and Jen was going to be taking over. It helped clarify the work Jen would be doing, and it helped her figure out if she wanted the job in the first place (thank God she did!). Be as descriptive as you can so you can evaluate the candidates objectively. You can Google other job descriptions if you need inspiration. Indeed.com and other sites are incredible resources. Use your ADORE list too!

Step 2: Be clear on what requirements are needed for the job

Don't cheat on the requirements. What education, level of work experience, time in the field, and so on do you need? If you need people to slot in and get moving, then hiring someone fresh out of school is not the way forward! They'll need training, and that takes time that you may not have. I've seen people be incredibly vague about requirements or not have any at all, and the new person was a disaster. There is great danger in having the wrong people apply. It wastes time reading resumes of people you'd never bring on!

Step 3: Define the CULTURAL elements that you want people to fit into

Jeff knew how to define his culture at Amazon. Do you know yours? Cultural elements are things like being family oriented, prioritization-driven, competitive, supportive, progressive, performance-driven, at ease with accountability, and the like. Even if you're an "army of one," you have a culture that requires clarity so you can explain it to those wanting to work with you.

Write down the important cultural elements of the business or team you want to build or strengthen. Ask around to see if people who know you and work with you have other contributions. Taking the time on this will have the biggest impact on the quality of people you bring into your world and the ease by which they slot in.

Step 4: Be clear on how you want them to think

How do you want them to process information? Do you need critical thinkers and problem solvers, or order takers (there's a place and time for both)? Do they need to be able to negotiate in difficult situations? Do they have enough experience so they don't get beat-out in competitive situations by their more experienced counterparts?

In my agency days, I had people on my team who needed to follow client instructions on content and style but had creative license to execute their work using their talents and skills. They had the ability to combine creative thinking and time management to meet all the deadlines *and* deliver great work. I needed them to be able to do both, and my agency ran like clockwork.

How do you need your people to think? Write down some ideas in your GOAT-book!

Step 5: Test before you hire

I love testing potential new hires. I fudged my way through so many interviews in my past, I know how unreliable they are! When I was hiring a Facebook ad analyst, I told prospects that I would do a Zoom meeting and they could bring up their Facebook analysis reports to show me what they've done. Two people sucked or were so arrogant I wouldn't hire them if they were the last people on earth. Aaron, in Tel Aviv, was perfect and continued to be perfect until the last gasps of my agency. He was an outstanding person and great at what he did. Giving him that test made me feel confident that I was hiring the right person.

Think of tests that you can offer that ensure that the person is right for you, things like:

- Spelling and grammar: give them a sheet with questions to answer, then leave the office for ten minutes.
- Technical capabilities: do a test in real time and have them do something within the system they say they're comfort-able with.
- Analysis: just like I did, have them create a report, but in real time, with you sitting there or virtually on Zoom

In your GOAT-book, write down an awesome test that will keep the Dragons away, letting only fellow GOATs rise to the surface!

Step 6: Don't go it alone

You only see things from your own perspective, so you need other people to observe and offer their input. This will also prevent you from making emotional decisions.

Sometimes, if someone looks and talks like us, we immediately think they *are* us, but they're not. Hiring based on likeability is dangerous, and having other people in the room or part of the process helps manage those emotions and avoid disaster.

With this final step, in your GOAT-book, write down whom else in your organization you'd bring in to help you hire the right people. If you have a small team, or no team, find people with good decision-making and have them there to vet the candidates.

NECESSARY CONVERSATIONS – AND NECESSARY ENDINGS

Ah, tough conversations. I have more clients who avoid hard discussions than those who actively seek them out. But your approach and attitude about tackling tough decisions or ending something completely is important. You can let someone go from your work or from your life. You could be ending a strategy that hasn't worked or changing streams to focus on work more aligned with what you want. Change is everywhere, but we often shy away from engaging in the conversations or endings necessary to bring it about.

If someone is working for you, but clearly not working out, dragging everyone along as if all is hunky-dory isn't helping. The better thing, the kinder thing, is to offer them an opportunity to find something more aligned with their own GOAT.

There are two things we will explore, and they mostly go the same way:

1. Necessary conversations
2. Necessary endings

Dr. Henry Cloud's book *Necessary Endings* is clearly where I've gotten inspiration for this section. But while I know things must end, sometimes we need to just have hard conversations, without necessarily ending anything. I've grouped these two situations together because the process of preparing, executing, and being emotionally ready is the same.

First, let's explore why we avoid these things in the first place.

- We hang on too long and feel committed because of the time invested
- We are afraid of the unknown
- We fear confrontation and conflict

- We are afraid of hurting someone
- We think we may be viewed as being "mean"
- We are afraid of our own sadness once the ending or conversation is over
- We don't have the skills to end things with grace
- We don't have the words
- We've experienced so much pain already that we don't want more

I'm sure you can add to this list, but at least you get the point. We avoid things mostly because we're not emotionally ready for them. As we move through the upcoming steps, you'll find ways to ensure that you're strong from every angle before you even set foot in the door with whomever you need to talk.

Step 1: Accept that there are life cycles and seasons

Everything in our lives happens in seasons and cycles. What worked ten years ago cannot work the same way today because so much has changed. To hold onto unrealistic ideals simply because "it's how it's always been done" is insane and will get in the way of your ability to live a full and meaningful life.

We biologically change as we age. When women hit menopausal age, the maternal caring part of our brain diminishes to almost nothing. Men become more sensitive. Our needs change. Industry, economy, and political stages change. Everything has a life cycle, and each season has a set of strategies that work best, particularly when they depend upon other people, systems, or structures to work properly. You may start a business and wear all the hats, but eventually you have to hand over some of the work. You can't please everyone and meet all *their* most convenient timelines. At some point, you have to speak up for yourself or you'll be run ragged, having no time to live your own GOAT life. The simple act of accepting the cyclicality of life will help emotionally get you to the position where hard but necessary things must be done.

Step 2: Accept that life produces too much life

You will always have more …

- Relationships than you can nurture
- Clients than you can service all in the same way

- Mentors who once "fit" but whose time has passed
- Partners and people who need all your time
- Strategies than you can execute
- Physical stuff than you can have room for and can store

Life produces too much of everything; at some point, some-thing has to go. It's not that these things suddenly aren't important. They played a key role in your life and where you are today. But that doesn't mean they're right for tomorrow.

Step 3: Accept that incurable sickness and evil exist

This is a sad but true fact. You need to know when to cut evil and toxicity out of your life. These people sometimes aren't even aware of it, and even if you point it out, their poison within may be too much for them to accept it. Energy-sucking people may exist in the world, and your job is to ensure they're not in *yours*.

They need to be let go to find a place where they are more likely to thrive. If they are toxic to your culture, you, your team, or anyone who is part of your world, the best thing for everyone is to cut ties, and quickly. The longer you wait, the longer their poison will seep into your organization. One day, those who you count on will leave *you* because they can't deal with the toxicity anymore.

These people will take your time, money, effort, and energy and will never want to change. Most often, they have adopted a very strong identity around how they act, and they will defend that identity viciously. They're not happy, but they don't know who they'd be without their misery. If they refuse to be helped, then being removed is the only option.

Step 4: Begin with the end in mind

When tackling something hard but necessary, the more prepared you are the better. Now that you've accepted the reality of the situation, it's time to get down to the conversation! You begin by clearly outlining how you want the situation to *end*. This ensures emotions or arguments don't derail you during the talk. Write out what you want to say ahead of time in as great detail as you can. Use bullet points, phrases, or sticky notes that you arrange on a wall. It doesn't matter how you do it; what does matters is that you know how you want this conversation to end before you begin, and work back from there.

You cannot control the person you're talking to, but you can control yourself, what you say, and how you come across. Think of your GOAT self outlined earlier; maybe you can define a GOAT self when it comes to necessary conversations and endings! That way you have a clear road map for how to act, think, gesture, and talk. You can even write a series of statements that start with, "I want to leave the conversation ..." to cover all possible directions the discussion can take.

Step 5: Remove emotion

Emotions are your friend until they're not. If you're afraid of hurting the person you're talking with, you have to bolster your resolve so you don't falter in the conversation and try to "make things work." If you're not clear on how you feel, then you risk being sidelined by the other person's feelings. The emotions of the person across from you may be far stronger than yours, and their Dragon may come out swinging. In order to not be swayed from your decision, emotions need to be noted and tamed ahead of time.

Get in touch with your two sides:

- Your concern for the other person
- Your concern for the truth

If someone is truly not right for your group, then that is the truth and it must be your guide. Truth needs to win the day. Write out "truth" statements that you can use as your tethers, keeping the conversation in control and moving toward the conclusion you know is best.

Step 6: Validate the person

Validating and acknowledging the other party and the powerful emotions they may be experiencing calms them down. I've done this with my kids as they entered their teens because I wanted to have decent conversations, even if they were freaking out. If they got mad, I'd say, *"I can see that this is making you angry."* Before I tried that out, I figured they'd just get even more mad at my rather obvious statement. But they didn't. Their anger and frustration started to come down, and we could actually talk about what was going on. Validating someone is to see them, truly. It will help them manage through the emotions they're dealing with and ratchet down the big ones.

You may also find it helpful to validate their reactions through the conversation:

- "I can see that this is making you upset."
- "I can see that you may not agree with how things have turned out," and so on.

The more you validate, the more they will calm down and avoid saying or doing things to make their situation worse. You don't change your mind, but you can acknowledge that the conversation is a tough one.

Step 7: Get agreement

At the end of the conversation, make sure they know what was said and what comes next. Things like:

- "What have you heard me say?"
- "I want to be sure you are going away with a good under-standing of the situation and of each other."

If they distort your words, reply with, "No, I am not saying (twisted thing). I am saying that I need to make this change for the reasons we've already talked about." Keep reiterating your truth over and over until they stop twisting your words.

Step 8: And finally, don't be squishy

At the point that you are having these conversations, you have decided on the ending or what you want to happen next. Don't make it hard for yourself by giving in and being squishy, back-tracking to "work it out." It *won't* work. By the time you've decided to have this conversation, chances are you've given them every opportunity to fix things, to no avail. Things have to change. When Ashley was having a hard conversation with someone, she said she did it with "ice in her veins," not because she wasn't emotional, but because she had found the resolve to avoid backing down, no matter what the other person did or said.

Here are some final tips:

- Leave no wiggle room
- Let there be no false hope
- Do not soften the bad news with falsehoods

Because you'll just have to do it again ... and you don't want to do this again.

TAKING CARE OF YOUR HEALTH AND WELL-BEING

Last but not least, take care of yourself. GOATs do this religiously. Ray Dalio credits his massive success to it, as do Bill Gates and other big guns. Even little guns do this! I'd be nowhere if it weren't for my daily gym regimen. It gets all my frustrations out, makes me feel strong, and gives me energy for the entire day. Without it, I'm sluggish and slow.

Taking care is only hard if you don't have a strong sense of self-worth. As you remedy that situation, you'll find that you look for opportunities to rest, rejuvenate, and be more clear-headed, ready to dive right back in. You *have* to take the downtime. It's non-negotiable.

Luckily for you, you get to define what "downtime" means. We all have varying levels of energy. I know some folks with long COVID who have to carefully manage their energy because they run out faster than they used to. You may have health considerations that make some movements difficult. Or gut situations that make food hard to digest.

As this book draws to a close, I want you to make one final commitment, not to me, but to you and your future self.

I want you to commit to listening to your body and your mind, taking the signals you're given and instead of pushing them away, investigate them. They are your GOAT calling to you, imploring you to work in a way that brings you immense satisfaction every day, without resistance and pain.

Every business book I've ever read talks about personal care, slowing down, and taking a break. If you're super busy and a week's vacation or even half a day off is too much, then take micro-breaks. Practice "release tension/set intention," which only takes two minutes. Take three conscious breaths. You can do it anywhere, any time.

For the last time, get out your GOAT-book. Make a list of things you will commit to doing this year, which count as rejuvenation time. It's not "down" time — it's time to think, reflect, and let some of the ideas just beneath the surface rise to the top. Stare at the water or a blank wall. The greatness within you is trying to get out, and you can shove it back into its cage by being simply too busy to listen.

Your Dragon will always be waiting at the door, ready to pounce and take over. Don't let it. Build the strength of your greatness, your goodness, and your superpowers. Be willing to do the work and to challenge how you've always thought. Evolve strategies to suit your desired outcomes. Give yourself permission to stop doing things counter to how you're wired.

This is all self-care: doing what is good for you. Not familiar, but *good*. Comforting, not comfortable. Sustainable, not susceptible. And as your GOAT grows in strength, value, emotional stability, and power, the Dragon that used to keep you back simply fades quietly into the background, and there's no sound except your breath and heartbeat to remind you it's even there. The big, bad emotions that you used to shove down and avoid become your allies and friends. They are useful and lead you to being a better, more well-adjusted human. They are good. Everything, in fact, is good.

There is only one way to know which one of the two will win, your Dragon or your GOAT …

The one that wins is the one you feed

ABOUT THE AUTHOR

Rebecca Mountain runs a High-Performance Coaching firm whose mission is to remove the obstacles people put in their way, so they can take full advantage of their inner greatness. Her work combines the principles and methodologies across multiple disciplines, weaving them together to form customized solutions so her clients can live happier, wealthier and more fulfilled lives. She lives in Burlington, Canada with her husband and the one kid (of four) still in high school. The other 3 are attempting to adult.

A free ebook edition is available with the purchase of this book.

To claim your free ebook edition:

1. Visit MorganJamesBOGO.com
2. Sign your name CLEARLY in the space
3. Complete the form and submit a photo of the entire copyright page
4. You or your friend can download the ebook to your preferred device

Print & Digital Together Forever.

Snap a photo   Free ebook   Read anywhere